LEADING CHANGE
in Your World

LEADING CHANGE
in Your World

Larry M. Lindsay
Mark A. Smith

TRIANGLE PUBLISHING
Marion, Indiana

. Triangle Publishing

Leading Change in Your World
Larry M. Lindsay and Mark A. Smith

Direct correspondence and permission requests to one of the following:
Email: info@trianglepublishing.com
Website: www.trianglepublishing.com
Mail: Triangle Publishing
                1900 West 50th Street
                Marion, Indiana   46953
                USA

Scripture quotations are from the following sources:

Authorized King James Version (KJV), 1611.

Contemporary English Version (CEV), Copyright © American
Bible Society, 1995. Used by permission.

The Living Bible (LB), Copyright © Tyndale House Publishers.
Used by permission.

The Amplified New Testament (ANT), Copyright © The Lockman
Foundation 1954, 1958, 1987. Used by permission.

Lindsay, Larry M. and Smith, Mark A.
Leading Change in Your World
ISBN: 978-1-931283-24-3

Third Edition

Printed in the United States of America

TABLE OF CONTENTS

ACKNOWLEDGMENTS

Many people contributed to this book and the result is a compilation of their ideas. A special thank-you to our wives, Gail and Debbie, and our families for giving us the time we needed for this endeavor. Your support was wonderful. To David Wright we say thanks for the dream. To Publisher Nathan Birky of Triangle Publishing, thank you for believing in our project and guiding us every step of the way through each edition. Thanks also to Bobbie Sease for her outstanding editorial work and to Juli Knutson for proofreading the original manuscript. Again, we would like to thank Gary Phillips and his team for their significant contribution to the first edition, as well as Lyn Rayn and Chari Rhoads for designing and formatting the revised editions.

Additionally, we thank the members of the initial idea and review committees for their time, support, creative input, and helpful critique: Clarence L. "Bud" Bence, Jerry Brecheisen, Keith Drury, Sharon Drury, Robert Hamill, Bill Millard, Steve Resch, and Keith Studebaker.

Most of all, we give thanks to God for inspiring us to initiate this project and for helping us to complete it.

Larry M. Lindsay
Mark A. Smith

PREFACE

By government standards, I grew up in a socially and economically disadvantaged family. We may have had the necessities of life, but we did not have the nice things of life. My parents considered education past the secondary level a luxury. The typical resident of my small southern town was destined to work at the local lumber factory. These parameters defined my world. By age fourteen, I knew that if I were to break out of this world, I would need to change it. I saw education as the key.

Even at that young age, I began to form a plan with specific goals. I wanted to obtain a bachelor's degree, followed by a master's degree, and then a doctoral degree. I wanted to be a teacher, then a principal, and finally a college dean. I wanted to write a book and build a church. And I wanted to accomplish all of these goals by the age of thirty-five! As long as I was dreaming, I might as well "dream big." Despite an automobile accident that left me unable to walk for nearly a year and required me to undergo multiple surgeries, I accomplished those goals—by age thirty-five. How was this possible? With God's grace and a good plan, I was able to change my world.

By world, I do not mean the world globally, but the world in which you operate each day: your family, your neighborhood, your workplace, your church, your community. Many people feel helpless about changing their worlds, backing away from even the smallest adjustments in their lives. Because they lack knowledge, planning skills, or leadership abilities, they fear the outcome of change. Concepts like "strategic plan" and "goal implementation" terrify them. It is "safer" to deal with the known, they reason, than to venture into the unknown.

It is my hope that this book will *change your view of change*. Co-author Larry Lindsay and I hope to accomplish this by giving concrete, real-life examples of change in process. By personalizing our change concepts, we bring the theoretical world down to earth, putting faces, hands, and feet on the principles we employ to help you effect change. Throughout this text, you will encounter real people and real situations—either from our own experiences or from others with whom we have interacted over the years. In some cases, names, places, and details have been adjusted to ensure anonymity.

We approach this challenge with a Christian worldview, recognizing that God is in the business of changing lives, capable of transforming people into what He created them to be. With that model to guide us, we want you to see that by changing your world, you ultimately can change the larger world around you.

—MARK A. SMITH, ED.D.

INTRODUCTION

Leading Change in My World

It is no mystery that people and organizations in the world are in great need. Just try asking people how much of their time is spent dealing personally with needy or urgent issues at home or at work. Many will indicate that they are being affected by the forces of change in their lives, that they often sense a lack of control over situations. Too many times they find themselves managing by panic rather than by plan. They want a greater degree of life-balance. And, they want to be of greater help to others.

The frantic pace of change in a chaotic world tends to keep us spinning out of control, stressed and feeling as if we are being driven rather than driving. And change keeps picking up speed. If you thought you could manage healthy change in the world, or at least within your circle of influence, would you be willing to try? If you were inspired, able and equipped to manage change in your life in order to help others make change in their lives or organizations, would you do so?

Never in the history of America has there been greater opportunity to be a world changer. There are great needs among individuals, families, neighborhoods, schools, churches, businesses and service-based institutions. Jesus demonstrated how to meet such needs in these words:

When I was hungry, you gave me something to eat, and when I was thirsty, you gave me something to drink. When I was a stranger, you welcomed me, and when I was naked, you gave me clothes to wear. When I was sick, you took care of me, and when I was in jail, you visited me.   Matthew 25:35-36 CEV

No conscientious world changer can have total peace while there is sickness, addiction, depression, family strife, illiteracy, prejudice, misery on the job, racial strife, exploitation, greed, deceit, violence, killing, war and famine in the world. There is tension between a sense of joy in the presence of the Spirit of love, and living in a world so often devoid of it. The way to a more joyful and enriching life is:

"Instruct them to do as many good deeds as they can and to help everyone. Remind the rich to be generous and share what they have."   1 Timothy 6:18 CEV

The primary purpose of this book is to help you change *your* world so you can lead change *in* the world; to help you move from self-satisfaction to service as you relate to individuals and organizations within your circle of influence. This book will provide you with the inspiration, techniques and strategies to bring about positive, significant change in your world. We hope to inspire and equip you to make a greater difference in the lives of people.

We challenge you to "seize the opportunity" to do good deeds when the need is so great and ever present. It is time to change the way we manage change. The goals of this book are to:

- help you to know or clarify your life mission;

- enable you to achieve life-balance and a greater sense of contribution and service;
- inspire "change resisters" to become "change agents";
- help you to envision and foster a better world in your circle of influence;
- encourage you to influence change in your organization;
- help you to develop a strategic plan to facilitate change in order to do your best for the world; and
- stimulate you to do all the good you possibly can—to be rich in doing good deeds.

When meditating on being an agent of constructive change in the world I often read and reflect upon what is quoted often and attributed to an unknown monk penned centuries ago:

> When I was a young man, I wanted to change the world. I found it was difficult to change the world, so I tried to change my nation. When I found I couldn't change the nation, I began to focus on my town. I couldn't change the town and as an older man, I tried to change my family. Now, as an old man, I realize the only thing I can change is myself, and suddenly I realize that if long ago I had changed myself, I could have had an impact on my family. My family and I could have made an impact on our town. Their impact could have changed the nation and I could indeed have changed the world. (Unknown Monk, circa 1100 A.D.)

Each of us can play a significant role in making a difference in our world as an agent of constructive change. Indeed change is an inside-out process as indicated in the message of an unknown monk. We invite you to be the real change leader the world desperately needs today.

—LARRY M. LINDSAY, ED.D.

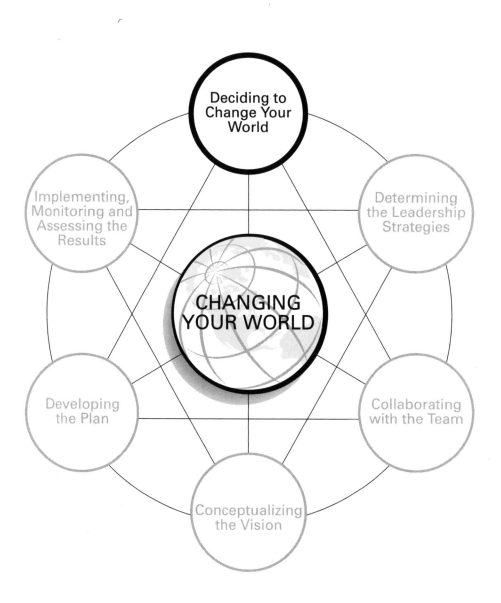

1

CHANGING THE WORLD—
Who, Me?

*"The more you change, the more you become
an instrument of change in others."[1]*

∽ *Howard Hendricks*

A Woman with a "Heart" for Change

Andrea Grossman started with a red heart sticker and changed her world. In little more than twenty years, she changed the world of those around her. Mrs. Grossman's Paper Company is now one of the world's largest manufacturers of decorative stickers, with more than three hundred fifty designs available in thousands of stores in the United States and Japan. The $1,700 she initially borrowed from her sister resulted in $20 million in recent sales, averaging a 15 percent increase in sales each year. Building on and expanding her idea for the red heart sticker, Mrs. Grossman's Paper Company now prints 15,000 miles of stickers a year—enough to circle half the globe.[2]

Based on the financial and statistical data alone, this is a remarkable success story. But Andrea Grossman's vision to change her world was predicated on "uplifting people in a positive way,"[3] presenting a model of excellence and cultivating the artistic talents of average, entry-level workers. In addition to sound financial principles, she was committed to building her company on the principle of "People First." This is evidenced by one hundred fifty employees who work in a relaxed, family-style environment, with corporate values that reflect Andrea Grossman's personal values.

In every dimension of life, people are confronted with change.

How did she break out of the simple lifestyle of a small stationery storeowner and become a world-class corporate leader? She started by meeting a specific need. A client expressed a desire for a red heart sticker, something she couldn't find anywhere. At this point Andrea could have shrugged and done nothing. Instead, she personally designed a red heart sticker and then filled her client's order by manufacturing them herself. With the success of these stickers, demand increased. Mrs. Grossman's Paper Company successfully weathered a flood of copycat companies in its first decade of existence. Expanding and diversifying its product line assured this company's place as an industry leader in the following decade.

THE "CONSTANCY" OF CHANGE

Someone once quipped, "Change is inevitable—except from a vending machine."[4] More poignantly, someone else said, "If nothing ever changed, there would be no butterflies." Both statements underscore the "constancy" of change. In defining the word "change," *Webster's Dictionary* focuses on four aspects:[5]

1. Change—to make radically different; to give a different position, course, or direction to; to transform; implies making either an essential difference often amounting to a loss of original identity or a substitution of one thing for another

2. Alter—implies a difference in some particular respect without suggesting loss of identity

3. Vary—stresses a breaking away from sameness, duplication or exact repetition

4. Modify—suggests a difference that limits, restricts or adapts to a new purpose

Some people resist change, like the film star who battles the aging process through multiple surgeries. Others welcome change, seeing opportunities for growth and improvement.

However, if there is a particular aspect of change that alarms people today, it is the speed at which change is taking place. In the last century we moved from an industry-based society to a technology-based society. Where it once took two to three decades for

Those who view change as an improvement can be termed "World Changers."

3

major organizational and cultural change to take place within an industrial framework, it now takes only two or three years for major change to occur within technological parameters. Many experts claim that information is doubling every seventeen to thirty-six months, intensifying this phenomenon of accelerated change.

Leading Change: Action or Reaction?

Accelerated change overwhelms some people, causing them to feel powerless over circumstances they cannot seem to control. Others seem to thrive on change, anticipating its challenges and adapting its benefits to their personal and professional lives.

World changers refuse to be controlled by perplexing circumstances.

Those who view change as a negative force can be termed "life takers," people who *take life* as it comes to them, who shrug their shoulders because they can't find any red heart stickers. Life takers *take from* rather than *add to*; criticize rather than innovate; dwell on the problem rather than seek the solution; project negativism instead of optimism; tend toward self-centeredness instead of being service-minded.

Conversely, those who view change as a positive force can be termed "world changers." They see opportunity instead of obstacles. They figure out a way to make things better in their relationships and actions. They recognize that our rapidly changing world needs people with better ideas, quicker responsiveness and a willingness to change.

In responding to change, human beings seem to walk between these two extremes. They either manage change or they let it manage them. King Whitney Jr. said:

Change has considerable psychological impact on the human mind. To the *fearful*, it is *threatening* because it means that things may get worse. To the *hopeful*, it is *encouraging* because things may get better. To the *confident* it is *inspiring* because the challenge exists to make things better. Obviously, then, one's character and frame of mind determine how readily he brings about change and how he reacts to change that is imposed on him.[6]

Figure 1.1

A QUICK SELF-ASSESSMENT

LIFE TAKER	WORLD CHANGER
Fearful, Threatened	Conficent, Inspired
Incapable, Dependent	Capable, Empowered
Procrastinating, Desperate	Motivated, Encouraged
Stymied, Unwilling	Willing, Eager
Lethargic, Apathetic	Ready, Energized

If we visualize these negative and positive aspects of change on a continuum, we can characterize the "fearful-threatened" aspect of the *life-taker* at one end, and the "confident-inspired" aspect of the *world changer* at the opposite end. Most of us can be found somewhere in the middle, trying to balance change with a "hopeful-encouraged" frame of mind. Where do you see yourself on this continuum? (See Figure 1.1.)

World changers refuse to be controlled by unwanted and unplanned change or perplexing circumstances. For instance, they do not wait for issues of neglect or conflict to "go away," because they know from experience that this is an ineffective means of dealing with problems. They seize the opportunity to create constructive change.

World changers anticipate change. They take the initiative to confront and conquer any issues that diminish their sense of well-being or that interfere with their quality of life. Moreover, in their words and actions world changers help others change their world.

Dream Wider and Higher

Your influence on the world around you is based largely on your willingness to *expand your vision*, allowing you to see change as an opportunity and not as a threat.

In *Leading Change*, John Kotter identifies several characteristics of effective change, among them:[7]

1. **Necessity**—In order to maintain a competitive edge, organizations and individuals must see that change is necessary.

2. **Urgency**—If change is to occur, a sense of urgency must propel the individual or company to action.

3. **Vision**—Vision molds and clarifies the need for change and assists in structuring implementation.

4. **Communication**—Communication translates the vision and enables it to take effect.

5. **Teamwork**—Change is best realized when individual talents and strengths are combined.

To be successful in the next decade, people and organizations—businesses, schools, government, faith-based or nonprofit institutions—must develop a plan to deal with the reality of accelerated cultural change. They will have to think more clearly, work smarter, dream wider and higher, and relate to one another in different and more efficient ways.

On an individual basis you must ask yourself: In what ways am I outdated in my thinking, education, life skills, and job effectiveness? How does this limit my ability to influence my world in a positive way? If I must change, how and what must I change? Can I manage change and still carry on without too much disruption to my life?

A MODEL FOR CHANGE

Acknowledging the rapid pace of change, as well as the need for a well-designed plan to deal with it, Alfred North Whitehead said: "The art of progress is to preserve order amid change and to preserve change amid order."[8] A fast-paced culture requires a model that enables people to manage change.

The purpose of this book is to offer such a model. Figure 1.2 illustrates a plan to help you move from a passive, "life-taking" status to an active, "world-changing" presence in all areas of your life—as well as the lives of others.

As you examine the Change Model, you will see that six interrelated/interdependent circles revolve around the center circle (Changing Your World). These we call the **change elements**:

- Deciding to Change Your World
- Determining the Leadership Strategies
- Collaborating with the Team
- Conceptualizing the Vision
- Developing the Plan
- Implementing, Monitoring and Assessing the Results

FIGURE 1.2

A MODEL FOR CHANGE

The change elements represent the objective strategy to bring about productive change. Outside a larger circle around the change elements are six capitalized words. These we call the **change concepts**:

- Imagination
- Illumination
- Destination
- Determination
- Coordination
- Culmination

The change concepts represent the intuitive-feeling dimension of change. Change requires a confluence (a coming together) of these change concepts and change elements, a blending of subjective/ creative thinking and objective/strategic planning.

Examining the Concepts of Change: The Outer Circle

In every invention there are two creations—the idea of the invention and the invention itself. The first begins in the heart and mind of the inventor or architect. Preceding the physical or material process of creation is the intuitive or imaginative process of creation.

Every human being has a measure of *imagenuity* (i.e., the genius and creative imagination of God, the Creator of the universe). At times we are captivated with a sense that there may be a better way to do something. We become intrigued with this possibility until it becomes a fascination.

> *"I think and think for months, for years. Ninety-nine times the conclusion is false. The hundredth time, I am right."*
>
> —Albert Einstein

1. Imagination

Fascination leads to the decision to implement this better way. You begin to ask yourself, how can I perceive this situation differently? What is the best way to alter this relationship? What will this change bring me in return? You move from fascination to **imagination.**

Einstein said, "Imagination is something more important than knowledge." He also said, "I think and think for months, for years. Ninety-nine times the conclusion is false. The hundredth time, I am right."[9]

2. Illumination

As you begin to tap into the enormous power of creative imagination, you are drawn toward a compelling opportunity. You begin to write the vision. As you write the vision, you sense that you are beginning to crystallize your thoughts about how you might accomplish this feat. You move from imagination to **illumination.**

3. Destination

The vision helps you determine the goals and action steps you need to take to move the invisible creation into the visible realm. A critical step in shaping the unseen, illumination involves generative thinking and strategic planning. The writing of goals and action plans enables you to see clearly where you are going, how you will get there, and how you will know you have arrived. Illumination leads to **destination.**

Once you have developed a strategic plan in the invisible dimension, you have charted your destination. As you move from the unseen to the seen, destination gives you focus and empowers you to push forward.

4. Determination

At this stage you may have compiled a "to create" list and charted your plan of action. You sense that you are involved in an important process, a process that will help to create something worthwhile. You see that your goal is entirely within reach. This sense of intrinsic value coupled with attainability spurs a fighting **determination** to fulfill the dream or vision—to see the project to the end. As you begin the project, you move with determination and establish dominion over your vision.

5. Coordination

In the creative process, the visionary or innovator must understand the importance of coordination. Distractions, hindrances and obstacles clutter the path of an individual setting out to change his or her world. Often the greatest enemies are your own thoughts and feelings—especially when you experience resistance or when the going gets tough. It is at this point that you must underscore your fighting determination—using the coordinated synergy and collective intelligence of a team to overcome these obstacles or distractions and prevent them from derailing your vision and strategic plan. Coordinated action enables the team to override setbacks, mistakes and thoughts of quitting. It means meeting such challenges with tenacity of purpose, while remaining flexible and open to adjustments or alternative methods of completing the plan. When you are able to do this, you move from **coordination** to culmination.

6. Culmination

Whether you are building a house, writing a book, completing a course or reconciling broken relationships, there is a sense of great joy as you approach the finish line. The closer you get to the completion of a big project or to the accomplishment of a worthwhile goal, the greater your sense of fulfillment. For many, the culmination of the project not only fills them with gratification but also with humility as they sense God's hand in this worthy endeavor.

It is at the point of culmination that you must take time to celebrate, thank and recognize the team members involved in the journey. The point of culmination also should be a point of beginning. This is no time to stifle the creative process! As you have worked toward your stated goal, you may have been inspired to pursue tangent goals; many times a good idea generates other good ideas. For example, as you seek to improve one company department, you see how other departments can benefit from similar changes. Culmination points to a spirit of renewal and a commitment to continuous improvement. It confirms that you stayed the course and got the job done well.

MAKING IT PERSONAL:
Doing Something about Paper Waste

One woman's example clearly demonstrates how change can have a rippling effect. Disturbed by the large quantity of paper thrown away daily at her office building, Clare remarked to various employees that the company should initiate a recycling program as a way to "save the trees." Clare was environmentally conscious but, as a staff member in a building with one hundred employees, did not feel she had the "clout" to change the status quo. Still, the waste of such enormous quantities of paper bothered her—so much so that she finally decided to come up with a plan. This involved calling a local recycling company to find out what would be involved in placing recycling bins at strategic areas within the office building.

Clare then enlisted the support of key office staff members around her and explained her ideas about a recycling program. She asked for a meeting with her leadership team and presented her plan, identifying the primary reasons for recycling wastepaper and offering ways to implement an effective recycling program. Upon review of her presentation, the leadership team agreed to the plan and gave approval for the entire division to begin recycling wastepaper in the building.

One inspired staff person challenged the status quo (*imagination*) and fulfilled her own dream to "save the trees" (*illumination*). In charting a course (*destination*), she changed the world of one hundred individuals around her (*determination and coordination*) — uniting them and enlarging their vision of how to help the environment (*culmination*).

Examining the Elements of Change:
The Inner Circle

From the change concepts located on the outer circle of the change model (Fig. 1.2), we now move to the six circles inside. These change elements represent the objective strategy to bringing about change, as well as an effective, realistic approach to managing change:

- Deciding to Change Your World
- Determining the Leadership Strategies
- Collaborating with the Team
- Conceptualizing the Vision
- Developing the Plan
- Implementing, Monitoring and Assessing the Results

Each element is related to and interfaces with the other elements. Together with the six **change concepts,** these **change elements** comprise an effective, realistic approach to leading change in your world.

1. Deciding to Change Your World

It might seem daunting to learn that only a small percentage of the population can be classified as world changers. Sadly, most of us are life takers. Many drift along taking what life throws at them. Many fail to take responsibility for their own lives and live without purpose or direction. The prevalent societal philosophy seems to endorse this lifestyle, assuring us that we are not responsible for our actions, attitudes and circumstances. Instead, we are pacified into believing that we are just products or victims of our circumstances. Our "appropriate" response then is a sense of betrayal and injustice.

MAKING IT PERSONAL:
A Different Perspective

Randy didn't buy into that kind of thinking. Raised in a poor African-American community of the inner city, he refused to believe in everyone's assessment that he was worthless. Looking around at his surroundings, he decided to change his world. He did that by making the decision to attend a local community church. Even as a teenager actively involved in the congregation, he began to impact the lives of many. He later became a respected and influential leader in the community. Randy didn't leave the inner city. He served on the city council, led a drug awareness campaign, and literally saved many youngsters from a life of crime. By staying, Randy became an instrument of change in his world.

The decision to change our world begins with just that—a decision.

The decision to change your world begins with just that—a decision. Many times the difference between the haves and have-nots, the leaders and the followers, the world changers and the life-takers is simply the willingness to make a decision and take the first step. We will examine the process of decision making more closely in chapter 2.

The decision to change your world doesn't have to be focused on something "world-sized." It can involve something as simple as making a lifestyle change, incorporating more discipline or exercise into your daily routine, taking a course to improve your job skills, or reaching out to the community through volunteer work. All of us have areas that need improvement and all of us can benefit from change.

2. Determining the Leadership Strategies

Even the best strategic plan will accomplish nothing if it lies dormant. A plan is only effective if someone—like a Clare or a Randy or an Andrea—takes a leadership role, ensuring that the plan becomes a project. In chapter 3, we will compare and contrast some leadership models. Of the many good leadership models developed over the years, all require the leader to be involved in implementing the plan. Whether a coalition needs to be built, an agency contacted, a proposal written or a plan developed, passionate leadership propels the project and inspires those who are involved in the project.

3. Collaborating with the Team

In sports, the idea of teamwork is critical. Teams that stress the contribution of every team member rather than the importance of one superstar are usually the most successful. The same is true in other realms: personal, family, church, political, voluntary or public service, small business or the corporate world. Getting the right people involved in a strategic plan, creating a shared vision, focusing their energy and talent, and holding them accountable to the vision are the most effective ways to implement change. We will study techniques for developing an effective team in chapter 4.

4. Conceptualizing the Shared Vision

Once you make a decision to change, you must formulate a vision for the change area. This is the time for some creative, visionary thinking. Some people call this "blue sky" thinking because the sky is the limit when it comes to a vision. Visionary thinking encompasses such ideas as health, happiness, opportunity and peace for everyone. A vision may be as large as beginning a company and developing it into a multibillion-dollar international corporation. It may be as small as building a better mousetrap. It may be as universal as writing a book, or as personal as obtaining a college degree. Regardless of the perspective, the key is to conceptualize the vision and allow it to crystallize in your mind. Without a vision, any plan of changing the world cannot succeed. Developing a vision is the subject of chapter 5.

5. Developing the Plan

Having crystallized your shared vision, you must create a strategic plan. Creating a plan involves these key steps:

- Identifying a critical need or compelling opportunity
- Making a decision to initiate a change
- Creating a personal mission statement
- Identifying core values
- Setting goals for the area of change
- Writing action steps to accomplish the goals

We will discuss these key steps in depth in chapter 6.

The importance of a strategic plan cannot be overemphasized. The difference between world changers and life-takers is that life-takers seldom create a plan. This is true in the corporate world as well.

Organizations that have a strategic plan for mapping future goals and endeavors are purpose-driven organizations. They succeed because their strategic plans involve shared vision, creative thinking and collective analysis. In fact, by taking the time to prepare a strategic plan, these companies take aggressive steps to steer and control their futures, rather than be vulnerable to unanticipated future events. The same applies for individuals.

6. Implementing, Monitoring and Assessing the Results

After the plan is implemented, the next step is to develop ways to assess the goals. Setting goals is important, but the goals must be monitored and measured for desired results, giving evidence of the impact of change.

Holding yourself accountable is the key to successful change.

It is in this area that most people fail. Holding yourself accountable is the key to successful change. For example, personal goals to change spending patterns as they relate to the family budget are all well and good. But if the goals are ignored, change will not occur. As simple as it sounds, this is the difference between success and failure. It doesn't matter how many lofty goals a corporation or individual sets if there is no way to measure their effectiveness. All goals must be assessed periodically. The primary purpose of assessment is not only to look at how goals are achieved, but also to allow room for the reevaluation or redesign of goals. Based on what the assessment reveals, adjustments and changes should be built into the strategic plan. You will learn ways to monitor and assess your goals in chapter 7.

Processing Change

In writing of planned change, Gregory Moorhead and Ricky Griffin inform us, "Organizational development is the process of planned change and improvement of the organization through application of knowledge of the behavioral sciences."[10] Industrial psychologists confirm that the process of planned change and improvement in organizations also applies to self-directed growth and development.

Intrapersonal and Interpersonal—How They Relate

The process of change first begins with *intrapersonal* (i.e., personal or professional) goals. Every capable individual should be responsible for regularly initiating personal or professional change. As individuals manage change in their own lives, they are preparing themselves and serving as models for change in various *interpersonal* and organizational spheres of influence. People who effectively manage themselves are in a better position to lead others.

George Bernard Shaw wrote, "I rejoice in life for its own sake . . . Life is no brief candle to me. It's a sort of splendid torch which I've got hold of for the moment, and I want to make it burn as brightly as possible before handing it on to the future generations."[11]

Change starts with an individual and spreads throughout the culture of a group or organization. As one enduring proverb puts it, *"Any enterprise is built by wise planning, becomes strong through common sense, and profits wonderfully by staying abreast of the facts"* (Proverbs 24:3-4 LB).

Becoming a World Changer

Earlier, we defined the purpose of this book as offering a model to help you lead productive change. As subsequent chapters follow the pattern of this model (Fig. 1.2), it is our hope that you will find information and inspiration that will enable you to translate effective change in your personal life to the lives of others— enabling you to become an "agent of change" in your world.

> *As individuals lead change, they are preparing themselves to serve as models.*

Take a moment to reflect and really think about the people and organizations in your world. Focus on three great pains in the world:

- the pain of disconnection
- the pain of apathy
- the pain of regret

We encourage you to invest in the self-discipline and change actions that will enable you to lead others out of the pain of disconnection, apathy and regret.

Becoming a world changer will require dedication to a plan. If you follow each part of the model and complete each section, you will discover that the emerging truths reflect the purposeful plan that was there all along. The important question is, "Are you ready to change?" Are you ready to impact the lives of those around you, your church, company or organization? If so, begin leading change in your world!

Endnotes

1. Howard Hendricks, *Teaching to Change Lives: Seven Proven Ways to Make Your Teaching Come Alive* (Portland: Multnomah Publishers, 1996), 20-21.
2. Louis R. Carlozo, "Achieving Excellence, Family Style," *Life @ Work*, Vol. 3, Number 2 (March/April 2000): 11.
3. Ibid.
4. Found at www.home.att.net/~quotations/christian.html
5. *Merriam-Webster's Collegiate Dictionary,* 10th ed. (Springfield, MA: Merriam-Webster, 2001), 190.
6. Robert H. Rosen, with Lisa Berger, *The Healthy Company: Eight Strategies to Develop People, Productivity, and Profits* (Los Angeles: Jeremy P. Tarcher, 1991), 95.
7. John P. Kotter, *Leading Change* (Boston: Harvard Business School Press, 1996), 21-23, paraphrased.
8. Peter J. Laurence, *Peter's Quotations: Ideas for Our Time* (New York: Bantam Books, 1977), 75.
9. Sheila Murray Bethel, *Making A Difference: 12 Qualities That Make You a Leader* (New York: The Berkley Publishing Group, 1990), 44.
10. Gregory Moorhead and Ricky W. Griffin, *Organizational Behavior: Managing People and Organizations* (Boston: Houghton Mifflin, 1998), 547.
11. Bob Buford, *Half Time*: *Changing Your Game Plan from Success to Significance* (Grand Rapids: Zondervan Publishing House, 1994), 59.

Learning Activities—Chapter 1

It is not where you start, but who you intend to become and what you desire to accomplish that makes one a transformational agent of change.

1. Obtain a spiral notebook or journal as you engage in your leading change journey. We want you to engage in deep-dive successful thinking (i.e., analytical, practical, creative, and reflective thinking) throughout your leading change journey. First, commence the process of reflective assessment by jotting some notes in your "Leading Change Journal." Jot down your responses to the following questions:
   a. As an action learner (i.e., transformational learner), what is the best I can imagine? Jot down four or five inspirational descriptors or behaviors.
   b. What are my strengths that add value in the workplace?
   c. What do I really like to do that adds value to others?
   d. What constructive change project would I like to accomplish if I had the time, skill sets, and motivation?
2. Identify two–five friends, class members or workplace colleagues and interview them. Since we learn a lot from listening, we want you to frame five or six questions you would like to ask colleagues. Please create the questions and make arrangements for conducting the interviews. Questions might include:
   a. What have I discovered that is new and interesting at the present?
   b. What is the most critical issue I am currently facing?
   c. What is the biggest challenge I am currently facing?
3. In what ways would I like to be healthier, happier, and more influential one year from now?
4. What lessons have I learned by taking the time to engage in deep-dive successful thinking and transformational learning aimed at personal mastery?
5. Emotion (passion: red-hat thinking) is a key driver for individuals engaging in real change. How do I honestly feel right now? Record your responses in your new "Leading Change Journal." (Let the journal remember so you won't forget.)

∽ Notes & Ideas ∽

✑ Notes & Ideas ✑

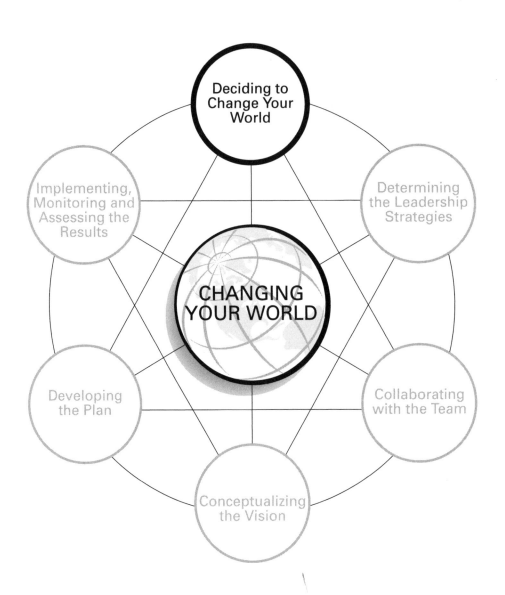

2

IT STARTS WITH A DECISION
Deciding to Change Your World

"In a higher world it is otherwise, but here below to live is to change, and to be perfect is to have changed often."[1]

      John Henry Cardinal Newman

A Time for Introspection

In Gail Godwin's *The Finishing School*, fictional character Ursula acts as an agent of change in the life of a woman named Justin. Ursula explains her insights on people this way:

There are two kinds of people. One kind, you can just tell by looking at them at what point they congealed into their final selves. It might be a very nice self, but you know that you can expect no more surprises from it. Whereas, the other kind keep moving, changing . . . they are fluid. They keep moving forward and making new trysts with life, and the motion keeps them young.[2]

Becoming Agents of Change

Change masters, pathfinders, visionaries, entrepreneurs, consultants, change facilitators and transformational leaders are some of the popular titles associated with being agents of change. The spirit of the role is to move

- from chaos to order,
- from stagnation to continuous improvement,
- from obsolescence to change,
- from tradition to innovation.

Change is a process through which an individual, unit or organization innovates, updates and increases productivity.

Change that is productive, enduring and deep-rooted has become the world's biggest and most persistent challenge. True change is at once technical and human, objective and subjective.

In the previous chapter, we looked at the dictionary definition of change. For our purposes in this book, we define change as a process through which an individual, unit or organization innovates, updates, increases productivity or improves performance. A change agent, then, is an individual who seeks to produce change or innovation in a unit or organization. Agents of change skillfully lead individuals to improved quality of life and help organizations achieve new goals. They effectively manage their own world and positively facilitate planned change for others.

> *Changing who you are now to who you think you ought to be is the decision to write a new story about your life.*

Earlier we explained that to be an agent of change in your circle of influence and a positive influence in the world, you must first manage change in your own life. That means using your passion, vision, creative ideas, core values and high-performing skills to help other people or organizations solve problems, develop opportunities, and plan innovation.

Agents of change cultivate resilience instead of complacency. Recognizing that it is far better to thrive than merely survive, they combat day-to-day challenges with energy, applying a spirit of renewal to even mundane projects. They demonstrate that stagnation or cynicism proves nothing and produces even less. And in this they learn something valuable: the smallest improvement can have a rippling effect, spreading to other areas and even generating other ways to improve. Innovative change strategies in the hands of vibrant people can make the world a better place.

James M. Barrie wrote, "The life of every man is a diary in which he means to write one story, and writes another; and his humblest hour is when he compares the volume as it is with what he vowed to make it."[3]

Ask yourself, "Are the challenges and pressures of change defining me? Or am I seizing the opportunity to choose who I want to become and how I want to define my role in the world?"

Changing *who you are now to who you think you ought to be* is the decision to write a new story about your life. It is to redirect your talents toward the purpose for which God created you. The story you write will detail how you move from merely *surviving to overcoming,* perhaps even *prevailing* in your circle of influence. It is a courageous step to redefine who you are and what you can accomplish if you are willing to use your power of choice creatively.

MAKING IT PERSONAL:
A Decision to Change

Eight-month-old Blake was diagnosed with retinoblastoma (cancer of the retina). This fast-spreading disease moves from the retina through the optic nerves to the brain. Once it reaches the brain, it can be fatal. In order to arrest the cancer's progress, doctors enucleated Blake's left eye. They removed his right eye when he was ten months old, leaving Blake totally blind.

At schools, Blake challenges students to change their worlds.

Blake's parents encouraged him to pursue the activities of any normal child. Blake learned to ride a bike—and at an even earlier age than his older brother. During his elementary-school years, he learned to snow and water ski. At the age of twelve, Blake decided to become a disc jockey. He applied for and was accepted into a radio broadcasting class at J. Everett Light Career Center, a career center for radio and communications classes in Indianapolis, Indiana. When he passed the Federal Communications Commission Examinations in Chicago, Illinois, he became—at the age of fourteen—the youngest certified disc jockey in Indiana.

Today, Blake is a trainer and customer service consultant for Bank of America. He regularly receives awards for top achievement in his department. He is also a weekend disc jockey for one of the most popular FM radio stations in Dallas, Texas. Invited frequently to speak at school assemblies in the Dallas Metroplex area, he challenges students to change their worlds. He was presented with the Mayor's Award and was recognized as a "Dallas Star" with a Dallas Citizenship Award.

Blake's circumstances did not limit his ability to function effectively in life. They did not dictate his place in the world. As a boy he made a fighting decision to change his world. Today as an adult he not only prevails in his circle of influence, he also impacts the lives of others—helping them change their worlds.

What Is My Circle of Influence?

Before making a decision to change your world, it is important to first assess your perception of the world as it is. Figure 2.1 illustrates the typical individual's Circle of Influence and the seven spheres or domains in which he or she operates. As indicated in the illustration, each of these spheres is affected by the others, just as your life is influenced by the interrelatedness of the various domains in which you interact. Total well-being results from maintaining a healthy life-balance in these seven interrelated and interdependent spheres of your life:

1. **Spiritual**—This domain concerns your perceived purpose in life, your relationship with God, and the ways you cultivate that relationship. We place the spiritual domain at the center of the circle of influence because we believe that your ability to function effectively in the world, to relate to others in your various spheres of influence, stems from the nature of your relationship with God. If that relationship is flawed, all other areas will be defective as well.

2. **Mental**—This domain concerns your interest in learning

29

new things and how you control negative thoughts.

3. **Physical**—This domain encompasses your lifestyle habits and how well you take care of yourself.

4. **Family**—This domain pertains to your family relationships, how you perceive your role in the family, and what things you do to nurture healthy relationships.

5. **Professional Growth**—This domain includes your perception of your worth, work habits, and plans for increasing your value in the workplace.

6. **Workplace**—This domain involves your performance on the job, your relationship with peers, and your level

FIGURE 2.1

CIRCLE OF INFLUENCE

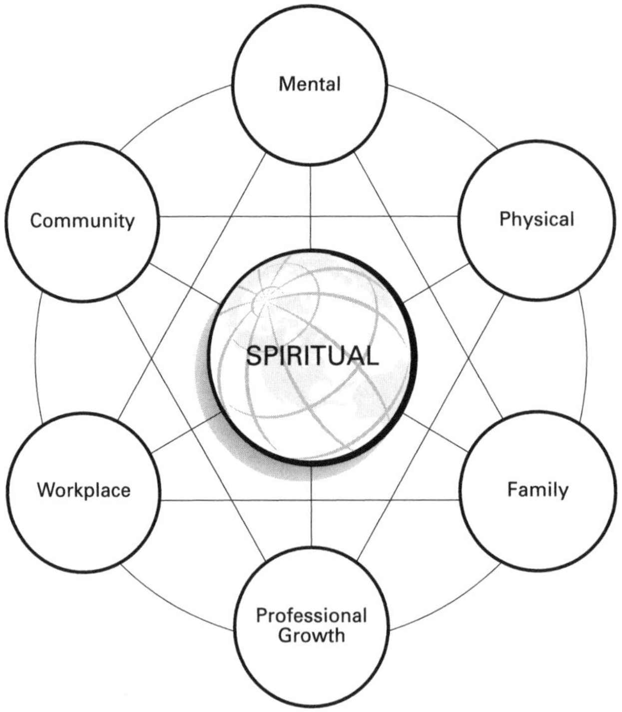

of satisfaction on the job.

7. **Community**—This domain includes your relationships with people and colleagues at work, as well as your involvement in service or church organizations, political groups, and other community service.

A Time for Self-Assessment

As the Circle of Influence (Figure 2.1) illustrates, the seven domains of your life are intricately interrelated in much the same way as the individual elements of the Change Model (Figure 1.2, Chapter 1). To initiate productive change in your world, you must make changes in each of the seven domains of your life.

To initiate productive change in your world, you must make changes in each of the seven domains of your life.

This begins by examining the areas of your life in which you have noticed the most changes during the past year. Ascertain whether these were unplanned, enforced, or planned changes. Having to share your office with someone whose office was damaged by a storm is an example of an unplanned change. A nonnegotiable company-wide pay cut at all levels is an example of an enforced change. Embarking on a family vacation is an example of a planned change.

If they were planned changes, determine if they resulted in a better quality of life, increased value in the workplace, improved performance or significant accomplishment.

Also check to see how vigilant you were in guarding against neglect, complacency and obsolescence in a fast-paced work culture. Ask yourself, "Am I happier, healthier, more at peace, more confident, more competent, more influential and better off today than I was a year ago? Do I have some compelling ideas that might enable me to improve the quality of my life and the lives of others I regularly come into contact with?"

To help you determine your strengths and weaknesses in the seven domains of your life, take a few minutes to complete the Self-Assessment Chart. (See Figure 2.2.)

Self-Assessment Chart

Directions: Thoughtfully conduct a self-assessment in the seven domains of your circle of influence. Depending upon your perception of yourself, write a 9 or 10 in the "Healthy Satisfaction Today" column; a 6, 7 or 8 in the "Slight Need to Change" column; or a 1 through 5 in the "Urgent Need to Change Column."

FIGURE 2.2

SELF-ASSESSMENT CHART

DOMAIN	Healthy Satisfaction Today (9-10)	Slight Need to Change (6-8)	Urgent Need to Change (1-5)
SPIRITUAL			
1. I have a clearly defined sense of purpose for my life.			
2. I have deep inner peace.			
3. I regularly read and contemplate inspirational works.			
4. I have a disciplined prayer life.			
Domain Total			
MENTAL			
5. I can control negative thoughts.			
6. I make time to think and meditate.			
7. I engage in hobbies and stay current on world events.			
8. I am a devoted lifelong learner.			
Domain Total			
PHYSICAL			
9. I practice good diet and nutrition.			
10. I am engaged in a physical fitness program.			
11. I know how to relax.			
12. I practice life-enhancing habits.			
Domain Total			

FIGURE 2.2

SELF-ASSESSMENT CHART continued

DOMAIN	Healthy Satisfaction Today (9-10)	Slight Need to Change (6-8)	Urgent Need to Change (1-5)
FAMILY			
13. I openly express my love for my family.			
14. I practice the Golden Rule by doing unto others what I would have them do unto me.			
15. I instruct, encourage and compliment my family.			
16. I spend quality time with my family.			
Domain Total			
PROFESSIONAL GROWTH			
17. I am investing in knowledge and skills for the future.			
18. I stay abreast of current knowledge in my profession.			
19. I regularly attend seminars or take courses.			
20. I am increasing my value in the workplace.			
Domain Total			
WORKPLACE			
21. I plan my work and work my plan.			
22. I regularly earn good performance appraisals.			
23. I look for ways to improve the work culture.			
24. I regularly experience the joy of productive work.			
Domain Total			
COMMUNITY			
25. I am actively involved in community betterment at work and in the neighborhood.			
26. I serve others through church and service organizations.			
27. I contribute time and money to the needy.			
28. I am involved in local, state or national government.			
Domain Total			

Complete Your Self-Assessment

Now that you have rated yourself, total each domain score and divide by 4. This will give you the average for each domain. To visually illustrate the high and low points of your circle of influence, we will ask you to transfer your average score from each domain to Figure 2.3, The Circle of Influence Assessment Wheel.

Directions: To complete the Circle of Influence Assessment Wheel, first average your scores for each domain in Figure 2.2.

Plot the average for each domain on the scale of 1 to 10 on the respective spokes of the Circle of Influence Assessment Wheel (Figure 2.3).

Summarize the Results

Study your self-assessment chart and the circle of influence assessment wheel. In what areas do you note strengths? Does this give you a sense of accomplishment or well-being? Do you feel especially good about your quality of life and do you see that you have a positive influence in certain areas? List three of your perceived strengths.

_____

_____

_____

_____

_____

_____

F I G U R E   2 . 3

CIRCLE OF INFLUENCE
ASSESSMENT WHEEL

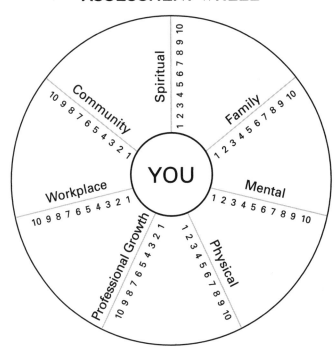

Now list the areas you believe demonstrate an urgent and compelling need for you to change.

_____

_____

_____

_____

_____

_____

Create SMART Goals

To help solidify the issues you wish to change, try perceiving them as SMART goals. A SMART goal is:

- **S**pecific—it doesn't target all your problems, but focuses on one issue at a time.
- **M**easurable—it falls within parameters that can be charted or measured for progress or setbacks.
- **A**greeable—my accountability partner, mentor, or team members fully support this goal.
- **R**ight to pursue—it is ethical, comes from pure motives, benefits others, and is the right thing to do.
- **T**ime-bound—the completion of the goal falls within a specified time limit, so that urgency is created and sustained.

In Your Mind's Eye

Writing a clear and concise SMART goal is the process of seeing the attainability of a worthwhile goal in "your mind's eye." A SMART goal should be

- a declaration of what you intend to do;
- phrased positively and in an affirming way;
- something you are passionate about;
- something that will benefit you and/or others.

Each of your goals should meet the criteria above. When you develop one or more of your own goals, your next step is to write a corresponding action plan—a method to facilitate the goal's achievement.

Choose an Action Plan

An action plan enables you to initiate constructive change in your circle of influence by detailing the steps needed to achieve your goal. An example might look like this:

SMART Goal: I will write ten chapters of a book by June 1. (Is this goal specific, measurable, agreeable, right, and time-bound?)

To achieve this goal, I have identified the following action steps:

1. In December, I will write my vision statement and book outline. I also will develop my strategy for writing this book, dividing the work into manageable portions.
2. I will begin researching and writing the first two chapters in January. When I complete these chapters by February 1, I will ask for the publisher's feedback.
3. I will continue to meet monthly with the publisher for assessment and editorial purposes. I will turn in chapters three and four by March 1.
4. I will complete chapters five and six by April 1 and respond to the publisher's feedback concerning the previous chapters.
5. I will complete chapters seven and eight by May 1.
6. I will complete chapters nine and ten by June 1. At our monthly meeting, the publisher and I will discuss the strategy for the second draft.

BENEFITS:

- The book will meet a compelling need.
- The book will change lives.
- The book will inspire, empower and equip people.
- The book will enable organizational change.
- The book will generate potential leaders.
- The book will contribute to a better world.

Write Your Own SMART Goals

As you make plans to increase a sense of well-being and value in the various domains of your life, remember the axiom: "Make no small plans for they have no power to stir your soul." (generally attributed to Nicolo Machiavelli) So be sure to set goals that will fire up the boiler room of your heart and stretch your comfort zone.

On the following lines write three SMART World-Changing Goals, the related action plans you envision for implementing these goals, and the benefits to be derived:

I CAN CHANGE MY WORLD GOAL AND ACTION PLAN
1. SMART GOAL

_____

_____

_____

_____

_____

ACTION PLAN

_____

_____

_____

_____

_____

_____

_____

BENEFITS

_____

_____

_____

_____

_____

_____

_____

_____

2. SMART GOAL

_____

_____

_____

_____

_____

ACTION PLAN

_____

_____

_____

_____

_____

_____

_____

BENEFITS

_____

_____

_____

_____

_____

_____

_____

3. SMART GOAL

_____

_____

_____

_____

_____

ACTION PLAN

_____

_____

_____

_____

_____

_____

_____

BENEFITS

_____

_____

_____

_____

_____

_____

A Life-Changing Mission

Personal or corporate change is a process—a progression from planning to doing, from immobility to mobility. The idea of "process" is important. Sometimes "doing" can simply mean being in a rut, doing the same unfulfilling, unproductive things over and over. A hamster running on its exercise wheel may appear to be "busy," when it actually is going nowhere. However, process implies forward movement. It is active, not passive, and looks to creating or being a part of something bigger and better. Before an organization can change, the people involved in the organization first must change. In order to understand more fully how to accomplish desired change, the organization develops a strategic plan. As we outlined briefly in the Change Model (Figure 1.2), a creative and inspirational part of that strategic plan is a mission statement and a clear vision statement.

Envision Personal Mastery

Personal mastery is imagining the best you can for yourself or for your team or organization. What indicators of personal mastery can you envision for yourself or for your team? Personal mastery indicators for an agent of change might include these:

1. Modeling the way
2. Being a lead learner
3. Developing mutual trust and respect with everyone
4. Doing your best work daily
5. Being an effective listener
6. Finding a better way every day to do something

Personal mastery for a team or organization might include these indicators:

1. A culture of collaboration and creativity
2. A mutually shared and acted-upon vision
3. A generative learning community
4. Courteous treatment of employees
5. Integrated systems
6. Excellent workmanship

7. Surpassing quarterly goals

8. Quarterly accountability coaching

If you were to be recognized as the "employee of the year" or "citizen of the year" or "mother or father of the year," what would you want significant others to say about you at the awards banquet?

Take a few minutes and jot down some notes regarding what you hope people would recognize in you. For example, would they say that you are trustworthy or someone who goes beyond the call of duty? Would you be considered a friend or colleague, an expert in your field, a go-getter, goal achiever and so forth? Make a list of ten or more qualities or attributes that describe you, things you would really hope to hear from a dear friend, spouse, your company president, the mayor or your pastor.

1. _____

2. _____

3. _____

4. _____

5. _____

6. _____

7. _____

8. _____

9. _____

10. _____

Now go back over that list and condense it into the top five. This list will begin to reflect your core values—the challenges you envision yourself mastering: the person you would most like to be.

1. _____

2. _____

3. _____

4. _____

5. _____

The Mission Statement: It's Not Just for Corporations

Profound individual or corporate change begins with a mission statement. One company that helps to train leaders explains the importance of a mission statement this way:

Creating a Personal Mission Statement will be, without question, one of the most powerful and significant things you will ever do to take leadership of your life. In it you will identify the first, most important roles, relationships, and things in your life—who you want to be, what you want to do, to whom and what you want to give your life, the principles you want to anchor your life to, the legacy you want to leave. All the goals and decisions you will make in the future will be based upon it. It's like deciding first which wall you want to lean your ladder of life against, and then beginning to climb. It will be a compass—a strong source of guidance amid the stormy seas and pressing, pulling currents of your life.[4]

Do you have a mission statement? If not, ask yourself, "What difference do I really want to make in my world?" A personal mission statement enables you to think about your potential influence in the world.

If you have never written a mission statement for your life's purpose, now is the time to accomplish that task. Doing this will give you a compelling sense of purpose and focus: who do you really want to be; what difference do you really want to make?

A personal-professional mission statement enables you to

1. draw from a power source greater than yourself (for Christians, that source is God);
2. make the world a better place in which to live, love, learn, work and serve;
3. discover your purpose for being;
4. realize your unique talents and full potential.

Let's take a look at some mission statements that others have written.

- My mission is to build a high-growth business that adds value to my employees and the customers we serve.
- My mission is to discover, model and teach enduring truths, helping others to experience a greater sense of life-balance, accomplishment and fulfillment in their lives.
- My mission is to please the Lord; to be a loving husband and father; to be rich in good deeds; to be fully productive in my work; and to be a difference maker in the world.

As you can readily see, a personal mission statement does not have to be a lengthy treatise! In fact, it should be brief and succinct.

In writing a first-draft mission statement, consider what you have learned about yourself from your two lists. Then review the mission statements above. If necessary, study some other mission statements. Many companies have their vision and mission statements prominently posted for everyone to see. Or check the Internet for the mission statements of various companies. Following that review, contemplate the person you most want to become and what you really want to accomplish in your life. Now, write your first draft. Be sure to make this statement clear and convincing. Include your primary actions. Focus on your impact upon people and your intentions to make things better for people and their organizations.

My mission is . . .

_____

_____

_____

_____

_____

_____

_____

_____

_____

_____

_____

_____

Study the statement you have just written, read it aloud a couple of times and ask yourself if this really captures who you ultimately want to be. Is your mission statement clear and convincing? Is it action oriented? Will it positively impact people? Is it focused on change—on making things better? Now write the second draft of your dynamic mission statement.

My mission is . . .

_____

_____

_____

_____

_____

_____

_____

_____

_____

_____

_____

_____

_____

_____

_____

_____

_____

Over the years we have helped hundreds of people write mission statements. Most people found the experience a bit awkward at first. But as they framed the mission statement and meditated upon the inspiring words, they felt a sense of knowing and becoming: the words projected who they wanted to become and expressed their desire to be empowered to make a difference in their world. As a result they were more passionate and effective in their spheres of influence.

As you change and improve, you will become a better example and a more capable initiator of productive change.

You have begun the process. We encourage you to make your mission statement a "work in progress." Write it in your day planner or on a 3 x 5 card, referring to it daily for a week or so. By doing this, you may find more inspiring or powerful words or phrases to incorporate into your mission statement. Keep developing and internalizing the person you believe you were created to be. As you perfect the wording, you will find that a mission statement is not so much created as it is discovered.

You Are an Enterprise!

As you change and improve, you will become a better example and a more capable initiator of productive change in your circle of influence. In this context, influence means to have a positive effect upon the knowledge, attitudes, values, beliefs, perceptions, behavior and performance of an individual, a group or an organization.

Over the years, educational psychologists and industrial psychologists have informed us that happiness is a choice. We can choose to be happy or miserable. We also have learned that employees who view themselves as self-employed, even when working for an employer, often will experience the joy of productive work. The polarity is: Do I have a life or does life have me? Do I have a job or does my job have me?

So why not declare yourself an enterprise, predicated on a joy-filled lifestyle! With your personal mission statement, SMART goals and action plans in hand, expand your vision to become *Changing My World, Inc.*

Wesleyan Leadership: A Decision to Love and Serve

Early in his ministry, John Wesley made a decision to love God with all his heart, mind, and body. And, he decided to love people. As a change leader Wesley transmitted a word of love, grace, redemption, renewal, and reformation to the people. And those people believed in Wesley as a faithful servant leader of God who genuinely cared for them. Yes, Wesley decided to love, know, and serve God in order to meet the needs of people. Given that decision to love and serve needy people, he became a world changer whose legacy and words continue to transform people and organizations everywhere.

Endnotes

1. Gerard Egan, *Change Agent Skills B: Managing Innovation and Change* (San Diego: Pfeiffer Publishers, 1988), 1.
2. Gail Godwin, *The Finishing School* (New York: Viking Penguin, 1985), as quoted in *Change Agent Skills* by Gerard Egan, 2.
3. John Bartlett, *Familiar Quotations,* 13th ed. (Boston: Little, Brown and Company, 1955), 791, quoting from James Matthew Barrie, *The Little Minister,* chapter 1, 1891.
4. Found at www.FranklinCovey.com. Accessed 3-26-03.

Learning Activities—Chapter 2

Creative imagination is a wonderful thing. Make a quality decision now to harness the potential of your creative imagination in becoming the best you can be for the world.

1. Complete the Self-Assessment thinking for real change assignments honestly and thoughtfully (pp. 32-35).

2. Given your reading, successful thinking, and assessment to date, identify two goals that you would like to accomplish. Write the SMART Goal, five–seven action steps, and the three–five perceived benefits in your text (pp. 38-40). You may want to transfer these to your new "Leading Change Journal."

3. What are key indicators of personal mastery for me? (Personal mastery is when I am at my best, bringing my "A" game to the issues, challenges, and opportunities of life at home, school or the workplace.) Write down seven–ten indicators of how others would see you when you are operating at your personal mastery level—the best you can be (p. 43).

4. Given the list of personal mastery indicators, go back over the list and condense it to your top five (p. 44). You may edit or modify the list to show the person you desire to be consistently.

5. What is my life mission (i.e., life purpose or life calling)? Jot down your current mission statement or first draft on page 46. Read it through two or three times and then write down your second iteration. It is important that you read your mission statement often, tweak it along the way, internalize it, and begin to live it out consistently well in all of your life roles.

6. Now that you have written, edited, and begun to internalize your mission statement, identify four–five core values that are consistent with and support your mission statement. See the examples. It is helpful to identify the four–five key values and briefly define each one. For example, Health: Health is the process of pursuing total well-being of spirit, soul, mind and body. Record your core value statement in your Leading Change Journal.

You have begun the process of transformation from who and what you are to who and what more you would like to become and accomplish. Congratulations! You have developed a personal and/or professional strategic vision (i.e., mission, values, indicators of personal mastery, and two goals to commence the inside-out change process).

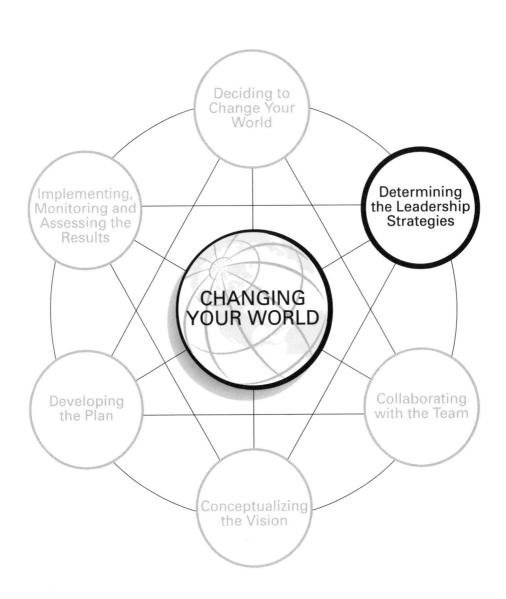

Deciding to Change Your World

Implementing, Monitoring and Assessing the Results

Determining the Leadership Strategies

CHANGING YOUR WORLD

Developing the Plan

Collaborating with the Team

Conceptualizing the Vision

3

FOREVER FOLLOWING, FOREVER LEADING
Determining the Leadership Strategies

> *"The servant-leader is servant first . . . It [servant leadership] begins with a natural feeling that one wants to serve, to serve first. Then conscious choice brings one to aspire to lead."[1]*
>
> ∞ *Robert K. Greenleaf*

Mine, mine, all mine . . .

Bart had a vision to change his world. The president of the company supported the vision. In writing the plan and goals, Bart even included how he would measure the goals. Although the project plan was in the works, there was one problem: Bart did not know how to lead the project. He always referred to it as "his" project. When meeting for group discussion of the plan's initiatives, he sometimes allowed others to give suggestions, but never included their ideas in the working plan. After two years the project failed. Why did this happen even with the support of the company's top leaders? The answer is that Bart's leadership strategies were defective. He did not understand the synergy of collaboration.

Leaders and Managers Are Not the Same

Tragically, outstanding leaders are in the minority. The emphasis in the last century has been on management issues—how to manage time, prices, goods, services—and management jobs. Copious amounts of literature still support this focus. But management and leadership are not the same things. Whereas management relates more to resources, leadership relates to people.

Managers are associated with the planning and organization of activities. They determine staffing levels, set performance standards, measure the results and determine if the standards are being met.

On the other hand, leaders are more concerned with an organization's forward movement. Planning is part of the job but the planning is related to vision thinking or strategic priorities. Leaders must set direction, share vision, mobilize forces, give purpose to the organization and empower others to manage.

> *Leaders must set direction, share vision, and mobilize forces.*

In today's information-based society there is a leadership deficit of crisis proportions. Companies, institutions and service organizations are looking for leaders who have character—who can be counted on to be men and women of trust and integrity. There are approximately three hundred million people in America and most are looking for compassionate, trustworthy leaders to help them change their world.

Jim Barnes, an authority on the subject of customer relationships, notes that leadership has many components, but "the most important has to be integrity and moral character."[2] He adds that leaders must be willing to sacrifice, plan carefully and surround themselves with quality people. Summarizing his thoughts, he says, "First-class people hire first-class people" and "a true leader is a servant of the people he leads."[3]

> *There is a critical shortage of change agents: men and women willing to accept the challenge to lead change.*

There is a critical shortage of change agents: men and women willing to accept the challenge to lead change in their families, their workplace, their community or in their church or synagogue. These same families, communities, churches and companies need a valiant response to the call of making a world-changing difference in the next decade.

Thus far you have made a commitment to change your world on a personal level. You may be thinking of the next stage: how to implement change in your circle of influence. In this chapter we will overview leadership strategies that will enable you to better structure and implement your vision for change.

Leadership Styles

Leadership theories or paradigms as they relate to organizations can be classified into four categories: managerial leaders, transactional leaders, and the two newest paradigms, transformative leaders and servant leaders.

While this chapter primarily will focus on a Servant-Leadership Model, it is important to understand how this particular model compares to the theories that have preceded it. We also hope to help you understand the contrasting roles of leaders within an organization. Most managers can become servant leaders, but servant leaders must identify the gift mix and core competencies of those they lead in order to accomplish the mission of the organization. The indicators we provide in Figure 3.1 and in the explanatory paragraphs below are not intended to denigrate particular leadership styles. Instead, these indicators are intended to enable agents of change to think about who and where they are in the leadership journey in order to achieve an optimum level of leadership effectiveness.

Figure 3.1	**Leadership Styles**	
Managerial Administration	**Transactional Leadership**	**Transformative Leadership Flowing into Servant Leadership**
Theory X Management	Theory Y Leadership	Theory Z Leadership
Micro-managing	Transactional	Transformative
Bartering	Bonding	Bonding & Binding
Distrust	Building Trust	Mutual Trust & Collegiality Permeates
Low Morale	Some High and Low	Consistently High Morale
Stagnation; Mediocrity	Growth & Improvement	"Prime" & High Achieving
Stressful	Creative Tension	"Flow"
Telling and Selling	Consulting & Cooperating	Team Learning & Co-creating
Lose/Lose	Win/Lose	Win/Win
Fixing Blame	Recognizing Mental Models	Systems Thinking
Low Performance	Professional Improvement	Personal Mastery
Giving the Vision	Getting Vision Buy-in	Shared Vision
Powerless; Robotic	Empowering	Empowered Change Agents
Builds Dependency	Mutual Interdependence	Autonomy; Self-directedness
Advocacy	Balancing Advocacy and Inquiry	Collaboration; Innovation

1. **Managerial administrators** tend to do what the CEO tells them to do. They direct the actions of the employees and place emphasis on order, control, and accountability. They tend toward informing and directing the work of employees, as well as rating and judging employee performance.

2. **Transactional leaders** understand the principle of bartering and negotiating in order to motivate workers to get the job done. This involves a focus on rewards, perks, and incentives. Task oriented and somewhat directive in their relationships with employees, transactional leaders advocate structures, systems, and procedures that produce high returns for the organization. They practice the principle that "what gets done gets rewarded." Transactional leaders also tend to evaluate employee performance.

3. **Transformational leaders** move toward a shared vision, team learning, and building a culture of mutual trust and collaboration. They focus on integrating the needs, personal goals, and core competencies of the individual with those of the organization. By recognizing the need to build upon the core competencies of the employees, they help to raise employees to higher levels of performance. Transformational leaders promote more team building, team learning, and team playing than most transactional leaders do. They believe that by enabling employees to activate all of their talents for the benefit of the organization, the

Leadership is enabling people to solve organizational problems.

employees also will experience a strong sense of fulfillment. These leaders are noted for high task orientation and consideration for employees. Transformational leaders tend to engage the employees in goal setting, reflective analysis, and self evaluation as much as possible.

4. **Servant leaders** are focused on the needs and interests of those they serve. They are builders of a collaborative community in which the employees are integrated into the shared vision and culture of the organization. Servant leaders focus on being the best they can be for the common good of those they serve and lead. By modeling the way, they encourage, empower, and equip employees to foster a shared vision, which results in continuous improvement of people and systems. They facilitate a process in which the work is purpose driven, meaningful, and rewarding to the employees as they serve the needs of clients. Servant leaders focus on valuing people, helping them feel special about who they are and what they do.

"Response-able" leaders will incorporate situational styles depending on the need and issue.

Leadership Defined

In *Leaders: The Strategies for Taking Charge,* Warren Bennis and Burt Nanus characterize leadership in this way:[4]

• Leadership is *authority*: Authority is the recognition and respect for the organization's board, for state and federal mandates, for the rule of law, for policy, and for negotiated contracts. When a leader understands legal and legitimate authority, he or she can act in an authoritative and responsible manner.

- Leadership is *vision*: Vision is seeing the achievement of the best the leadership team can imagine for a strategic plan, a new project, or the desired state of affairs for the organization over the next one to three years. Vision has a beginning and, once the strategic plan or the project is accomplished, it has an end. A shared vision is co-created, empowering and commiting people to create and act upon strategic and operational plans. A vision causes people to stretch and reach for the highest accomplishment possible.

- Leadership is *mobilization of forces*: To mobilize forces is to harness the human, physical, technical, and fiscal resources of the organization to support the corporate mission, core values, vision, and strategic plan. It is facilitating a shared vision, goals, and actions, empowering broad-based employee action to accomplish the plan created by a representative team of the organization.

- Leadership *commits people to action*: Committing people to action is one of the greatest challenges of twenty-first century leaders. Commitment grows out of building a generative learning organization that values, builds, empowers, and equips people to run with the shared vision and strategic plan of the organization. In this globally competitive and highly accountable period in our history, most organizations fail because they do not cultivate commitment to a shared vision or a culture of continuous improvement. The last thing an effective leader should ask the team or the employees is: Are we really committed to this vision and plan?

- Leadership involves *hard work*: Hard work, smart work, teamwork, and excellent workmanship are the fundamental actions of any top-performing organization. The challenge of leaders is to inspire and then unleash the enormous potential of the workforce. Leaders of championship teams and great organizations are wholly devoted to the best workmanship and highest quality performance possible. They constantly ask, "What are we doing well and where can we do better?" Outstanding workmanship ultimately benefits the people and the organization.

- Leadership is *associated with strength*: Leadership strength is often viewed as resolve and the ability to influence others. Outstanding leaders have a fighting determination to build the best organization possible for the good of the employees and the customers (clients). Leadership strength is demonstrated in the many tough calls they have to make, always keeping in mind what is the most fair and of the most benefit to all concerned. Leadership strength is demonstrated through one's character, will, ability, and passion to serve the people and the organization.

Leadership flows out of our being, doing and serving.

- Leadership is both *born and developed*: Leadership is both an art and a science, born and developed, objective and intuitive. It is true that some people have a leaning toward or gift of leadership. However, even these individuals must be involved in a lifelong leadership learning and development process. Current knowledge base, best practice, and innovations cause the leader to be the "lead learner," thus modeling the way of lifelong learning and professional growth for the organization. Leadership is a journey and one is always discovering new professional insights, principles, and practices that enhance the ability to be the best leader possible.

Richard Chewning offers these insights from *Business through the Eyes of Faith:*

Good business leadership is an art. It provides direction and purpose for an organization. It elicits trust and helps employees focus on the big purposes of the organization. Leadership must be earned. It is voluntarily given by those who follow, not taken by those who lead. Followers perceive that leaders can work with them to provide opportunities to meet their personal goals while making a contribution to the goals of the business.[5]

He adds that one of the most important aspects of leadership is recognizing that "each of us can grow and develop leadership skills."[6] In other words, each individual must develop leadership skills in order to change his or her world.

Getting Results—One Way or the Other

Daniel Goleman approaches leadership from a slightly different perspective, but with a similar inclination. "Leaders set strategy, they motivate, they create mission, they build culture." He says further that the "singular job of the leader is to get results."[7]

Unfortunately "getting results" is frequently misunderstood to mean a form of leadership that exploits and controls others. As we saw earlier, certain leadership styles (coercive, authoritarian) are more prone to this kind of distortion. In a seminar in Dallas, George Selig, Provost Emeritus of Regent University, explained three key words as they relate to leadership:

- **Authority** is the right to make decisions.
- **Responsibility** is the obligation to make decisions.
- **Accountability** is being evaluated on how authority and responsibility are used.

Leaders are always responsible to a higher authority, such as a board of directors. They are to be accountable for the decisions, actions, and performance of the organization. Effective leaders integrate authority and accountability into the job responsibilities of everyone in the organization. Without authority there can be no freedom of work flow through the organization. And without accountability there can be no means to measure the productivity of the people and the organization.

Many leaders fail to understand and appropriately use authority, responsibility and accountability. Effective leaders empower others. They delegate authority, responsibility and accountability to the trustworthy. And, they find mutually compatible ways to monitor and assess progress (get results).

Getting Results as a Servant Leader

To advance the field of organizational leadership, there is a compelling need for visionary leaders to comprehend the dynamics of human relationships under globally competitive conditions; to commit to building a collaborative culture of trust; to master the principles and skills necessary to lead a generative learning organization; and to possess the conceptual, creative, and collaborative acumen required to implement systems theory throughout the organization.

A servant leader influences people to collaboratively work toward mutually shared visions and goals in order to facilitate constructive change and produce results for the common good.

Within the parameters of this Servant Leadership Model, we define leadership as the act of modeling, serving and communicating the values, vision and goals of a community, team or organization in helping people solve real problems.

The Characteristics of Servant Leadership

Jim Laub defines servant leadership as "an understanding and practice of leadership that place the good of those led over the self-interest of the leader."[8] Laub describes effective servant leaders as those who:

1. **Display Authenticity**

   Servant leadership begins with a different view of yourself as leader. You are to be open, real, approachable and accountable to others. You are not higher than others due to your "position." In fact, position speaks to responsibility, not value. As you work with people within organizations, you will serve them if you display the qualities of authenticity.

2. **Value People**

   Servant leadership requires a different view of others. People are to be valued and developed, not used for the purposes of the leader. As a leader you believe that people have present value, not just future potential. People seem to have an innate ability to know whether or not they are being valued, whether or not they are being trusted. As a servant you accept people's value up front. You give them the gift of trust without requiring that they earn it first. As you work with people in organizations, you will serve them if you show them that you value them.

3. Develop People

Servants interact with others differently. Part of your responsibility is to help others grow towards their potential as servants and leaders. Therefore, you are looking to create a dynamic learning environment that encourages growth and development. As you interact with others, you are conscious of what you are learning together. The mistakes of others—as well as your own mistakes—are opportunities to learn. As you work with people within organizations, you will serve them if you show an honest desire to develop people (i.e., connecting with, encouraging, mentoring, growing, and equipping).

Servant leaders facilitate a collaborative community of trust and purpose.

4. Build Community

Servant leaders have a different way of looking at how people work together. You desire to build community, a sense that all are part of a loving, caring team with a shared goal to accomplish. Servants resist the tendency to "just get the job done." You are just as concerned with the relationships of the people doing the job. You know that people will be more impacted by the quality of relationships than they will be by the accomplishment of tasks. Therefore, you will intentionally work to build a community that works together and learns to serve one another in the process. As you work with people within organizations, you will serve them if you display the qualities of building community.

5. Provide Leadership

A servant leader leads for the good of those being led. Leadership is defined as Initiative, Influence, and Impact. The servant will not neglect to take appropriate action; in fact, leaders have a bias for action. This initiative-taking comes not from being driven by personal ambition, but by being called to serve the highest needs of others.

6. Share Leadership

Every leader has power and must continually make choices as to how that power will be used. The servant leader shares that power so others can lead, thus increasing the potential influence and impact of leadership.[9]

Practicing Leadership—from the Heart

Successful leaders do not emerge from a one-size-fits-all pattern. Just as individual companies differ in style, substance and method, so do individual leaders. Recognizing how to connect your style, strengths, vision and strategies to a particular project will go a long way in determining the project's success.

In their extensive research on leadership, James M. Kouzes and Barry Z. Posner note five key leadership practices that promote positive change:[10]

1. Challenging the Process (Status Quo)
2. Inspiring a Shared Vision
3. Enabling Others to Act
4. Modeling the Way
5. Encouraging the Heart

These five practices personify the essence of servant leadership. The spirit of this leadership style transmits a sense of trust and respect while influencing people to produce the intended results. This evokes a sense of appreciation, optimism, motivation, involvement, ownership and freedom to improve and advance.

MAKING IT PERSONAL:
From a Persian Palace . . .

The biblical character Esther is a good example of servant leadership. She first appears as Hadassah, an orphan Jewess. But, as Edith Deen points out, "four years later she rises to the position of a queen with amazing power, a power which she manages wisely."[11]

Despite her humble beginnings, Esther was placed in a leadership role and was then able to become God's tool to save the Jewish population from extermination. Deen highlights the leadership strategies that Esther modeled in leading the Jews out of harm's way:[12]

1. She gained favor with the people.

2. She used sound judgment.

3. She always thought of others first.

4. She offered to sacrifice her position and even her life to save others.

5. She was dedicated and loyal.

6. She exhibited virtuous character.

7. She was fearless.

8. She was prudent.

Esther's life offers a pattern each of us can follow. Could it be that the characteristics listed above might resolve the situation you so desire to change?

One of the greatest problems in the workforce today is the lack of leadership initiative from lower organizational ranks. While many companies or organizations are seeking ideas to resolve problems, few employees offer suggestions. Their reasons vary: some are afraid; some do not have favor; some have poor work habits; some do not believe their ideas are valuable or valued; and some do not care. And even more tragically, many managers are too controlling, too close-minded or too indifferent.

Esther changed her world. The question is, which of Esther's leadership strategies might work for you?

MAKING IT PERSONAL:
. . . to the Streets of Calcutta

Mother Teresa epitomized the idea of servant leadership

From a palace in Persia over 2,500 years ago, Queen Esther changed the lives of her people. In a more contemporary example, gentle, unassuming Mother Teresa brought the plight of Calcutta's street people to the world's attention. When she first walked onto those streets, the poorest of the poor were living and dying there. Many were lepers. Many were children. No one seemed to be doing anything about their desperate plight or deplorable conditions. Her heart was so moved by their need that she decided to take action to change the situation. She began to work as a "missionary of charity" with the lepers. In the book *Something Beautiful for God*, Malcolm Muggeridge says that Mother Teresa epitomized the idea of servant leadership by choosing "to live in the slums of Calcutta, amidst all the dirt and disease and misery."[13] He describes her as having a "spirit so indomitable, a faith so intractable, and a love so abounding, that he felt abashed."[14]

Although Mother Teresa is known for having changed the plight of many lives in the world, she went about her work one heart at a time. Love was the key to her tremendous influence. And woven through that love are several leadership qualities:

1. An outstanding work ethic
2. Concern for others
3. The ability to see a need

4. A vision to change the plight of the needy

5. A plan to implement her vision

6. The ability to organize resources

7. The ability to inspire the formation of the Mothers of Charity[15]

The Behaviors of Servant Leadership

In seeing a need and committing to meet that need, Esther and Mother Teresa changed their worlds. But the real victory is in HOW they accomplished their missions. Their leadership qualities were shaped by a spirit of humility and love.

Recently, a school superintendent shared his ideas regarding how dynamic leaders should lead in the public sector. He noted that the application of these principles had inspired his leadership team, the faculty and the school-community. He told us that great leaders transmit a compassionate spirit and exhibit the behaviors of a servant leader. In so doing these servant leaders provide the following:

1. Love and devotion as they encourage and strengthen others

2. Wisdom and good judgment as they guide and counsel others

3. Authority (caring and helpful influence) as they protect and support others

4. Goodness as they supply and comfort others

5. Equality as they work with others in the spirit of love and unity

If you are a servant leader, you have been promoted to a position of authority over those in your care. You must not use coercive and positional power to dominate people, nor should you act as a tyrant. A servant leader's role is to love, care, serve, train and empower those who are led.

How do you rate yourself? In those situations where you delegate authority, how are those leaders that you have empowered doing? What changes can you make to master or improve in these areas?

Inspirational Servant Leadership — President John F. Kennedy

In history's eyes, President John F. Kennedy will be remembered as an inspirational leader during the Civil Rights struggle of the 1960s. His ability to be a shining light in dark, troubling days inspired a nation to hope. Among the skills he used effectively were these:

1. The ability to create a vision
2. The ability to articulate the vision
3. A passion for excellence
4. The ability to motivate people toward a common cause
5. The ability to lead the cause

Inspirational Servant Leadership — President Ronald Reagan

President Ronald Reagan also will go down in history as one of the greatest inspirational presidents of all time. He was quoted as saying a worthy goal was "to have the vision to dream of a better, safer world, and the courage, persistence and patience to turn the dream into a reality."[16] This statement reveals his strong belief in the fact that one man could change the world. In fact, history already reveals that Reagan's belief system promoted action that led to the fall of communism.

> *Reagan had a strong belief in the fact that one man could change the world.*

Democracy prevailed through his determined, visionary and inspirational leadership. In *How an Ordinary Man Became a Leader,* Dinesh D'Souza points out that Reagan was governed by three basic elements of leadership:[17]

1. Vision—which gives the leader conviction and destination,
2. Action—the ability to get from here to there, and
3. Consent—the ability to articulate vision and rally the people.

From different political spectrums, Kennedy and Reagan inspired the nation with servant leadership that advanced noble causes and changed the world.

Defining World-Changing Leadership

A leader can stifle or liberate the talents and skills of the team or organization. After reviewing the various definitions, styles and strategies of leadership, we would define world-changing leadership in this way:

WORLD-CHANGING LEADERSHIP is the ability to identify compelling needs and envision solutions that require collaborative action, and to influence people and resources to create a better future. This leadership is an active, purposeful, skilled influencing of people to facilitate change or growth, enabling the team or community to achieve not only corporate goals, but individual goals as well.

With this definition of leadership, one becomes an active participant in making the world a better place. Rather than allowing the circumstances of life to control people, the leader influences positive action to control those circumstances. Leading coordinated action is the difference between being a life changer or a life taker.

Embodying World-Changing Leadership

In looking briefly at some well-known leaders in this chapter, we have identified certain characteristics and practices pivotal to effective servant leadership. Additionally, to effect substantive change in the world—to be a world changer— requires key strategies. As we focus on these strategies we would do well to study the Person even secular writers on leadership acknowledge to be perhaps the most influential leader of all time: Jesus Christ.

Jesus Christ had a vision. That vision was to change the world with a message of love.

World-Changing Leadership Involves Sharing Vision

Laurie Beth Jones suggests that "Jesus knew his mission statement, and he did not deviate from it. He declared that his mission was, in essence, to teach people about a better way of living." Further, in describing His leadership style she says that Jesus was "a leader who, like many of us, had to depend on others to accomplish a goal."[18]

Jesus Christ had a vision. That vision was to change the world with a message of love, one person at a time. A healthy, creative mind produces vision. Individuals and organizations are still in critical need of vision. Outstanding, world-changing leaders possess great vision. They change the seen and envision the unseen. Their creative vision convicts, inspires and enables people to achieve peak performance and attain extraordinary goals. That is exactly what Christ did as a leader. This is Jesus' vision statement as it appears in Matthew 28:18-20 CEV:

> *We must remember that world-changing leaders are preparing world changers.*

I have been given all authority in heaven and on earth! Go to the people of all nations and make them my disciples. Baptize them in the name of the Father, the Son, and the Holy Spirit, and teach them to do everything I have told you. I will be with you always, even until the end of the world.

With this simple vision statement the world was changed.

World-Changing Leadership Involves Developing Others

Jesus developed others by reproducing Himself in them. Great leaders transmit excellence by loving, serving and teaching their followers. As leaders develop those around them, they first must "manage themselves" by discipline. Followers will trust someone in

73

a leadership role who is disciplined and consistent in behavior.

We must remember that world-changing *leaders* are preparing world *changers*. Too many have conformed to society's standards and either have been changed by those standards or have become indifferent to the problems around them. Great leaders reproduce the leadership strategies of Jesus Christ in those they manage, teach and serve. The improvement, growth and spread of world-changing endeavors will occur in direct proportion to the supply of world-changing leaders.

World-Changing Leadership Depends on Integrity

Stephen Covey became a best-selling author by espousing the idea of "principle-centered leadership." He suggests that "principle-centered leadership introduces a new paradigm—that we center our lives and our leadership of organizations and people on certain true north principles."[19]

Leaders who commit themselves to world-changing endeavors will be faced with several critical issues:

- How do I lead from a balance of authority, power and influence?
- How do I use wealth and resources for constructive good?
- How do I enable people to solve societal problems?

Leaders must constantly safeguard against temptations to abuse these privileges. The way to protect oneself is through principled leadership and accountability. In our relatively short lifetime, we have seen many leaders fall because of their lack of accountability to God and to others. Even on individual projects, leaders must resist the tendency to promote themselves as the solution providers. This does not mesh with the character of Jesus Christ. His very character was the essence of "pure motives."

World-changing leaders are needed today, it's true, but only men and women of character—those who will advance a cause for the benefit of others.

An example of foundational Christian leadership principles can be found in this passage from 1 Peter 5:23 CEV:

> *Just as shepherds watch over their sheep, you must watch over everyone God has placed in your care. Do it willingly in order to please God, and not simply because you think you must. Let it be something you want to do, instead of something you do merely to make money. Don't be bossy to those people who are in your care, but set an example for them.*

Questions for Leaders

As you prepare to take leadership initiative for a project, ask yourself these key questions:

1. Do I really see a need before me?
2. Am I committed to hard work?
3. Am I committed to serving others?
4. Is there a project that I passionately want to pursue?
5. Can I enthusiastically share the vision with others?
6. Am I willing to take a risk with this pursuit?
7. Am I open to listening to the criticisms of others?
8. Am I ready to give fearless leadership?

9. Will this project allow me to model integrity?

The Legacy of Servant Leadership

Why was Jesus a great leader? After being with His disciples only three years, He had so profoundly ingrained His principles in them that an entire world was changed—and continues to be changed. Therefore, as leaders in a world-changing effort, we must constantly instill in those around us the desire to complete the job even after we are gone. Perhaps the greatest test of leadership is what happens after the leader is gone. Does the vision continue? Will the organization fail? In the case of Jesus Christ and Christianity, the ripples continue to spread! One man. Twelve men. And the world is changed.

Wow! What a leader!

Endnotes

1. Robert K. Greenleaf, *The Servant As Leader* (Indianapolis: The Robert K. Greenleaf Center, 1991), 7.

2. Dave Penticuff, editor, quoting Jim Barnes in "Integrity, Moral Character Critical in a Leader," *Chronicle-Tribune* (Marion, IN), 4 June 2000.

3. Ibid.

4. Warren Bennis and Burt Nanus, *Leaders: The Strategies for Taking Charge* (New York: Harper and Row, 1985).

5. Richard C. Chewning and others, *Business Through the Eyes of Faith* (New York: Harper-Collins Publisher, 1990), 133.

6. Ibid.

7. Daniel Goleman, "Leadership That Gets Results," *Harvard Business Review* (March/April 2000): 78.

8. Jim Laub, *Assessing the Servant Organization: A description of the six key areas and eighteen characteristics of the Servant Organization*, ©2000 Jim Laub, 1.

9. Ibid., 2-7, used with permission of Jim Laub and Bill Millard.

10. James M. Kouzes and Barry Z. Posner, *The Leadership Challenge: How to Keep Getting Extraordinary Things Done in Organizations*, from The Jossey-Bass Management Series (San Francisco: Jossey-Bass Publishers, 1995), 1-2.

11. Edith Deen, *All of the Women of the Bible* (San Francisco: Harper Collins Publishers, 1988), 147.

12. Ibid.

13. Malcolm Muggeridge, *Something Beautiful for God: Mother Teresa of Calcutta* (Garden City, NY: Image Books, 1977), 17.

14. Ibid.

15. Ibid.

16. Dinesh D'Souza, *Ronald Reagan: How an Ordinary Man Became an Extraordinary Leader* (New York: The Free Press, 1997), 228.

17. Ibid.

18. Laurie Beth Jones, *Jesus CEO* (New York: Hyperion Publishing, 1995), xvii.

19. Stephen Covey, *The 7 Habits of Highly Effective People: Powerful Lessons in Personal Change* (New York: A Fireside Book, 1990), 18.

Learning Activities—Chapter 3

Real change leadership can be learned if you have a desire to be more productive and make a difference in the world.

1. Constructive change leaders (i.e., Transformational or Redemptive Leaders) are often viewed as those who influence people. They put all of their talents into action for the benefit of the organization, the team, and the individual in attaining worthwhile goals. Carefully read and answer the questions on pages 75 and 76.
2. Given your present leadership perspective, what is your definition of leadership? Please record your leadership definition, as a real change leader in your world, in your Leading Change journal.
3. Reflective Assessment: What life lessons have I learned from reading this book and engaging in action-learning thus far? Please record your reflections in your Leading Change Journal.
4. How do you feel at this stage of your Leading Change journey? Please record your current emotions and reflective analysis in your Leading Change Journal.

∽ Notes & Ideas ∽

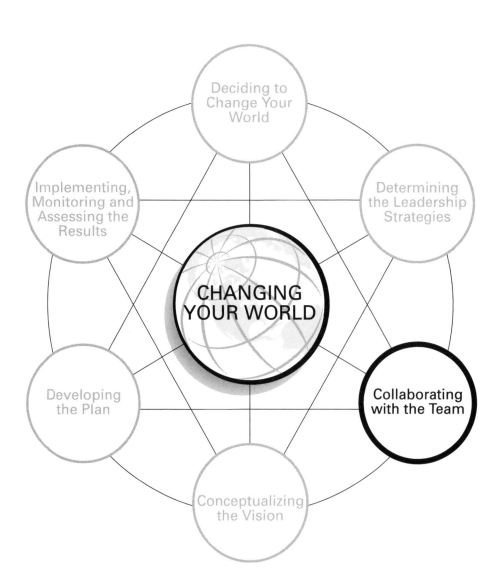

Deciding to
Change Your
World

Implementing,
Monitoring and
Assessing the
Results

Determining
the Leadership
Strategies

CHANGING
YOUR WORLD

Developing
the Plan

Collaborating
with the Team

Conceptualizing
the Vision

4

ALL TOGETHER NOW!
Collaborating with
the Team

> *"When highly motivated, confident,*
> *goal-directed, and resourceful team players are*
> *'carried beyond themselves,' your organization's*
> *competitive edge will widen considerably."* [1]
>
> ∽ *Bil Holton*

The Sum of the Parts . . .

Think of the last time you listened to a great orchestra or choir in concert. You might have been filled with awe as you observed the combined talents of such extraordinarily accomplished musicians and their conductors.

Adding to your sense of wonderment was the realization that this magnificent sound was made possible by the individual efforts of the members. Playing or singing together in harmony, these individuals produced something that epitomized the seamless, dynamic principle of unity.

The Principle of Unity

Unity results when the diverse talents and gifts of a group of people are combined for the benefit of others. Perhaps that is why the principle of unity has effected greater change in the world than any other principle. Unity stresses community and teamwork, with the emphasis on such words as "we" and "us."

Unity stresses community and teamwork.

During the creation of the world, God said, *"Now we will make humans, and they will be like us. We will let them rule the fish, the birds, and all other living creatures"* (Genesis 1:26 CEV). The focus here is not so much on the things that are created as it is on the Spirit of unity and harmony involved in the creation process.

Community will be a twenty- first century emphasis. The team concept, which stresses employee involvement, is a vital part of culture building. Teaming leads to a collaborative community, greater productivity and a sense of fulfillment among the people of a unit, department, company or organization.

Jon Katzenback and Douglas Smith define a team as "a small number of people with complementary skills who are committed to a common purpose, set of performance goals, and approach for which they hold themselves mutually accountable." In other words, they conclude, "Teams get results."[2]

Teaming: What It Means

Most employees and managerial leaders report that team activities are increasing in the workplace. Teamwork has become a key concept in nearly every field. Whether the team is a group of educators, a work team at McDonald's or an assembly team at General Motors, teamwork undergirds company policy and bolsters continuous improvement values. How well students, teachers and administrators work together determines the achievement level of a school. Whether a fast-food restaurant earns a reputation for great service depends on how well employees work as a team—sharing a common mission and sense of commitment to the job. And when every member of the team completes an assigned task at an automobile manufacturing plant, the consumer benefits from a higher quality product.

The "continuous improvement" movement initiated by the work of W. Edwards Deming and other quality experts incorporates employee involvement and teams as a core value.[3] Employee involvement teams such as managerial teams, self-managed teams, cross-functional teams, project teams, work teams, change facilitation teams and super teams permeate the literature of current business and organizational journals and textbooks.

Making a Greater Difference

Teams outperform individuals.

Katzenback and Smith studied teams in forty-seven organizations. Their conclusions revealed that teams outperform individuals and that team learning endures. The study further pointed out that teams bring together complementary skills and experiences that exceed those of any individual on the team.[4]

Teamwork provides opportunities for people to value the social and psychological gratification of empowerment and teamwork. There is a sense that "together we can make a greater difference" or "together we can change the world in our sphere of influence." Once

Once a team develops shared vision, it can accomplish unbelieveable results.

a team develops shared vision and worthwhile goals and once team members believe they are empowered, they can accomplish unbelievable results. Learning is explosive when a team, and not just one person, is involved.

In effect, success stems from being of one mind or unified as a team. Whether resolving perplexing problems, operating at optimum efficiency or creating quicker ways to execute and achieve goals, it takes teamwork to make it happen.

MAKING IT PERSONAL:
Teams—A National Priority

Shortly after the Gulf War, General Colin Powell wrote a manual entitled "Joint Publication #1," which was distributed more widely than any other manual ever published. Revealing a distinctive Powell touch, the language points to the value of teamwork, moral principles and the family or community model. Powell explains that the bedrock of successful organizations and units is "trusting people, working as a team, being a family."[5]

In this same publication Powell quotes General Dwight D. Eisenhower: "War is taking any problem exactly as you take a problem of your own life, stripping it down to its essentials, determining for yourself what is important and what you can emphasize to the advantage of your side."[6]

The essence is that making a plan and then accomplishing it through great team effort works not only in warfare but for individual or organizational improvement as well. As Eisenhower puts it, "We have got to be of one family, and it is more important today than it ever has been."[7]

Powell's publication focuses on such values as "integrity, competence, physical and moral courage that includes taking risks and tenacity, and teamwork built on trust and mutual confidence, delegation, cooperation, and cohesion."[8] His appreciation of team, community and family is further revealed in this statement:

> When a team takes to the field, individual specialists come together to achieve a team win. All players try to do their very best because every other player, the team, and the hometown are counting on them to win. So it is when the Armed Forces of the United States go to war. We must win every time. Every soldier must take the battlefield believing his or her unit is the best in the world . . . they must also believe that they are part of a team, a joint team, that fights together to win. This is our history, this is our tradition, this is our future.[9]

Teamwork—a creative synergy wherein the results are exponentially greater than the sum of the parts.

Yes, teams and a collaborative community of trust, respect and devotion are becoming the pillars of success in every field of endeavor in the twenty-first century. If we are to be effective as world changers in our sphere of influence, our future success will be a reflection of team learning and teamwork. There is a "multiplier effect" to teamwork—a creative synergy wherein the results are exponentially greater than the sum of the parts.

The Power of Teams

The Rochester Institute of Technology and *USA Today* jointly instituted the Quality Cup Award. This award recognizes individuals and teams in manufacturing, service, government, nonprofit institutions and small organizations who make significant improvements in their organizations. The Quality Cup Award stresses that quality begins with the individual and often results in dramatic team results. In the following vignettes of three Quality Cup Award winners,[10] look for ways that teams can bring about significant change in their organizations.

The Quality Cup Award stresses that quality begins with the individual.

Solving the Problem of Bad Steel

At one time General Motors and Ford threatened to cut U.S. Steel as their steel supplier. The problem: inferior steel. And not only that, the product repeatedly arrived late. Without management interference, a team of U.S. Steel union workers was sent out to examine the problems that bad steel was causing at customers' plants. Management gave the team freedom to change the system. As a result of their findings, the team suggested using rubber pads on flatbed trucks to cushion the steel, and plastic rings to protect the rolls from crane damage. They also persuaded other workers to take responsibility for the condition of the product by signing a tag attached to the shipment. Within a few years, rejected steel went from 2.6 percent to 0.6 percent.

Breaking a Bottleneck

When doctors ordered a computerized tomography (CT scan) or other radiological test at Norfolk General Hospital in Virginia, it took 72.5 hours to receive a written report. Three hundred to five hundred tests were ordered each day and the chief radiologist was embarrassed at the length of time it took to process the tests. A team of nine employees and managers studied the problem and identified fifty possible causes of delay. By further reducing the causes, they identified a few key areas that were creating eighty percent of the problems. Once they had uncovered these hidden bottlenecks, they upgraded the technology and eliminated fourteen of the forty steps in the process. As a result, the average time was reduced to 13.8 hours. The success of the team depended on the diversity of its representation and its commitment to defeat territorialism and to effect substantive change. Doctors reported that having information available to them more quickly allowed them to improve how they practiced medicine.

Identifying the Root Cause

A multitude of problems at Alabama's Wilkerson Middle School prompted administrators to attack the root cause: poor reading skills. Forming a team with teachers and students, they developed a radical solution—letting the children teach. The new program was called Readers Anonymous and matched struggling sixth graders with seventh- and eighth-grade students who could read well. Teachers worked in teams to identify "at-risk" students before they became academic problems, and met each morning before school to discuss students. The new culture created a climate in which kids and teachers wanted to come to school and learn more. As a result, reading scores jumped 21 percent for sixth graders, 31 percent for seventh graders and 26 percent for eighth graders over the previous year.

Team Emphasis

These three success vignettes emphasize the power and influence of teams as they bring about productive change in all types of organizations. It is likely that the initiative for significant change began with an individual and expanded to a team effort to produce the desired results.

Take a few minutes right now to think of a significant organizational change that you have observed. Who was the change agent for the project? What type of team was mobilized to do the joint planning and coordinated action? What were the results for the organization? What were the benefits for the change facilitation team?

The Purpose of Teams

Teamwork is the result of individuals working together in a spirit of agreement and unity to accomplish a shared vision and organizational objectives. Often teams enable ordinary people to accomplish extraordinary results.

A team accomplishes its objectives by focusing on three primary tasks. It must:

Identify
- Determine the problems or compelling need.
- Identify and clearly state the top priority problem or opportunity.

Analyze

- Collect the data.
- Find the causes and effects.

Solve

- Generate alternative solutions.
- Analyze the solutions and choose the best one possible.
- Develop the implementation goals and actions.
- Implement, monitor and assess the progress.
- Celebrate the achievement of the project.
- Renew.

Peter Senge suggests that " . . . virtually all the prime tasks of management [leadership] teams—developing strategy, shaping visions, designing policy and organizational structure—involve wrestling with enormous complexity. Furthermore, this complexity does not 'stay put.' Each situation is in a continual state of flux."[11]

Teams enlarge the thinking and expand the capabilities of the individuals while engaging in

- ongoing dialogue,
- problem identification,
- data collection and analysis (management of facts),
- analysis and decision making,
- strategic planning,
- plan implementation,
- overcoming obstacles and resistance,

- progress assessment,
- seeing the project through to its successful completion.

Choosing the Team

Whether the improvement goal and plan is targeted for an individual, a family, a community betterment project or a workplace project, the value of teams in achieving the ultimate success has been established. Selecting a compatible and effective functioning team is of paramount importance. The team should include individuals who

- recognize and believe in the need for change;
- will develop and implement the vision and goals;
- will wholly commit to successfully completing the project;
- are thinkers, doers and hard workers;
- are passionate about and dedicated to the cause or project;
- bring the diversity of thinking, experiences and skills to see the project through to completion.

It is easier for a team of people to remove a major obstacle.

While an individual initially may have identified the problem or suggested a solution, it will take a devoted team to complete the project successfully. It is easier for a team of people to remove a major obstacle in the pathway. Teams give the visionary a more focused, shared vision and the leverage to effect major change.

Establishing Team Leadership

Most teams have a leader or facilitator. Even in self-managed teams, a leader or facilitator will usually emerge. The team's performance will reflect the quality of its leadership. "Good leadership can best be seen among those who follow. Are they reaching their potential? Are they learning and serving? Do they achieve the required results? Do they change with grace? Do they manage conflict efficiently? If all of these are happening, you can assume that you've adopted the proper strategy for your organization's level of support."[12]

It is critical for the team to understand that results are an *expectation;* otherwise the team has little purpose in meeting and proposing a world-changing strategy.

Guiding Coalition

It is critical for the team to understand that results are an expectation.

An important step in building a team is to develop an understanding with key individuals regarding the ramifications and suggested goals of the project. Therefore, it is important for the team leader to build a guiding coalition or a core group to assist with the planning and design of the project. For the purposes of this book, this team is referred to as the *change facilitation team.* The identification of key individuals who are the "movers and shakers" of the organization is vital to the selection of the team. These key people are selected based on their ability to

- get things done,
- gather support for a project, and
- gain the attention of the top leadership if necessary.

In many organizations these key people are in leadership or management roles. However, it is important to note that some of the best projects are led by people in an organization's non-management roles. Of more importance than a person's position in an organization is that person's ability to *lead* the project once the design and planning have taken place.

A glaring example of deficiency in this regard comes from one organization's desire to upgrade its employee benefits. While this was a worthwhile effort, the project failed. No one from the personnel department had been involved in the team effort and, thus, the proposed changes could not be enacted or implemented. Without input on how the proposed changes can be implemented, any such project will fail.

Who Should Belong

In determining candidates for a guiding coalition or change facilitation team, James Shonk suggests including the following types of people:

- Managers who can commit resources and provide some degree of protection from budget cuts and other restrictions imposed by company practices and policies, and who also can provide support in the beginning and while the effort progresses.
- People with enough independence and authority to try new ways of operating. Plant managers who are away from corporate offices frequently fit this criteria.
- People with foresight who are able to see new ways of working and want to change the way in which the organization functions.

- Specialists from human resources departments who have expertise in managing change or know where to obtain it.
- "Influence" leaders who can help spread the effort's successes.[13]

Trust

Empowerment

Agreement

Mission

Skills

It is worth noting that many employee involvement efforts have been started at the lower levels of the organization, but failed to succeed because upper levels did not support these endeavors.

As you design your project and select your team, make sure to carefully consider the key persons to be involved. What are their strengths? What are their weaknesses? How will each person add to the team?

Successful Team Components

The team will experience success if the leader is careful in selecting and organizing the team. In addition to selecting the right people for a team, it is important to remember the key areas for which the team will be responsible. Dennis Romig identifies ten key areas or components of a successful team:[14]

Component	Benefit of Component
1. Team creativity	Having groups plan and problem solve promotes breakthrough performance only if the team uses creativity. Without creativity, a lot of time and

	effort can be expended with no payoff.
2. Team communication	Team communication skills, ground rules and norms create a supportive work climate that promotes creativity, breakthrough thinking, risk taking, and team member commitment.
3. Team meetings	Team meeting skills and structures harness the incredible energy available in group dynamics and produce high achievement in meeting goals. The team meeting is a mini-replication of the team's culture. Establish high-performance/high-commitment team meetings and there will be a high-performance/high-commitment culture. The energy of a highly charged participation and effective team meeting is contagious.
4. Conflict management	When employees are asked to bring their hearts and minds to work—to care and think about quality, productivity, cycle time reduction, and other workplace problems—there are conflicts. The conflicts can be healthy and result in breakthrough solutions when team members have effective and powerful conflict management skills.
5. Team mission	The team mission statement

establishes work priorities, unleashes the power of idealism, and aligns the team with the organization's mission.

6. Team goal setting

Effective team goal setting and action planning promote team member involvement and increase success and commitment.

7. Team roles and responsibilities

Roles and responsibilities are established and clarified regarding how each team member supports the other team members and the team's internal and external customers.

8. Team problem solving

Team members enthusiastically assume the role of solving problems together in and out of team meetings, instead of griping or bumping problems up to management. Using basic and easy-to-implement problem-solving steps, team members solve problems on the fly as they do daily work.

9. Team decision making

The most difficult of all team participatory management tasks is team decision making. Without decision-making skills, teams flounder, waste time, get in arguments, and end up requiring the manager to make the decision. However, when these skills are evident, teams make

	superior decisions and experience high commitment and rapid implementation of the decisions.
10. Work process improvement	Team members learn how to improve work processes. Work in all organizations tends to suffer from "bureaucratic creep," with process steps losing the value they had at one time. Team members aggressively look for ways to improve work processes and eliminate waste and cycle time.

Teamwork Means Collective Intelligence

Senge notes that the word team has the meaning of "pulling together." Thus, teams are described "as any group of people who need each other to accomplish a result."[15] Many organizations have utilized human development and group dynamics for team building, but have failed to institutionalize teamwork into day-to-day communication, shared decision making and joint problem solving.

Team learning leads to a collective intelligence that produces a "multiplier effect."

Arie de Geus, formerly with Royal Dutch/Shell Group Planning, noted, "The only relevant learning in a company is the learning done by those people who have the power to take action."[16]

Team learning leads to a collective intelligence that produces a "multiplier effect" within the unit, company or organization. Team learning is present when a team is chartered to become a collaborative community of trust with the goal of completing a major project or producing greater results.

What about Your Team?

As you prepare to conceptualize your vision and develop a strategic plan, have you thought about your team? Does it value the concepts of team learning and team playing? Does it exemplify the principle of unity, offering something greater than the sum of its individual parts? Does it face challenges *expecting* to succeed? Does it enable ordinary people to accomplish extraordinary results?

With that in mind ask yourself: Can your team engage in a shared vision, meet its objectives and create productive change in the unit, department or organization?

Questions to ponder:
Who should be included on the team?

_____

_____

_____

_____

_____

Who should lead the team?

_____

_____

_____

_____

_____

What is the team's purpose?

_____

_____

_____

_____

What are the team's goals?

_____

_____

_____

_____

How will the team determine roles and responsibilities?

_____

_____

_____

_____

Endnotes

1. Bil Holton, *Leadership Lessons of Robert E. Lee: Tips, Tactics, and Strategies for Leaders and Managers* (New York: Gramercy Books, 1999), 62.

2. Jon R. Katzenback and Douglas Smith, "The Discipline of Teams," *Harvard Business Review* (March/April 1993): 111-20.

3. W. Edwards Deming, *The New Economics for Industry, Government, Education* (Cambridge, MA: MIT Center for Advanced Engineering Study, 1993).

4. Jon R. Katzenback and Douglas K. Smith, *The Wisdom of Teams: Creating the High-Performance Organization* (Watertown, MA: Harvard Business School Press, 1993), 5-18.

5. David Roth, *Sacred Honor: A Biography of Colin Powell* (Grand Rapids: Zondervan Publishing House, 1993), 187-88.

6. Ibid., 187.

7. Ibid.

8. Ibid.

9. Ibid., 188.

10. James R. Evans and William M. Lindsay, *The Management and Control of Quality* (St. Paul: West Publishing Company, 1996), 473, citing *USA Today*, 8 April 1994.

11. Peter Senge, ed., and others, *The Fifth Discipline Fieldbook: Strategies and Tools for Building a Learning Organization* (New York: Currency/Doubleday, 1994), 266.

12. Linda Moran, ed., Ed Musselwhite, John H. Zenger, contributors, *Keeping Teams on Track: What to Do When the Going Gets Rough* (Toronto: Irwin Professional Publications, 1996), 74, quoting Max DePree.

13. James H. Shonk, *Team Based Organizations: Developing a Successful Team Environment* (Toronto: Irwin Professional Publications, 1997), 53-54.

14. Dennis Romig, *Breakthrough Teamwork: Outstanding Results Using Structured Teamwork*, ed. Kathy Olson (Chicago: Performance Research Press, 1999), 33-34.

15. *The Fifth Discipline Fieldbook*, 354.

16. Ibid., 355.

Learning Activities—Chapter 4

*Team leadership enables constructive change
to occur faster, better and to be more enduring.*

1. Think about the differences between team building, team playing, and team learning. When these three organizational learning tactics are coalesced into collaborative and coordinated action toward a common goal, continuous improvement and constructive change will follow. Brainstorm a list of seven–ten functional team behaviors. That is to say, what are the seven–ten team behaviors you believe should consistently be practiced by all members of a highly functional and high performing team? Write your thoughts in your Leading Change Journal.

2. What about the team you plan to work together with in a Leading Change in Your World project? There are five questions to ponder at the end of the chapter (pp. 97-98). Creatively think on these five questions and record your inspired thoughts in the text and transfer these to your Leading Change Journal.

∽ Notes & Ideas ∽

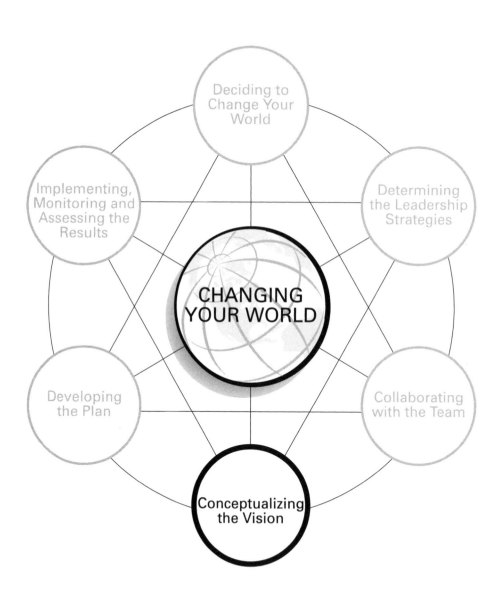

Deciding to Change Your World

Determining the Leadership Strategies

Implementing, Monitoring and Assessing the Results

CHANGING YOUR WORLD

Collaborating with the Team

Developing the Plan

Conceptualizing the Vision

BRINGING ORDER OUT OF CHAOS
Conceptualizing the Vision

"Where there is no vision, the people perish."

∞ *Proverbs 29:18 KJV*

A Natural Progression

Lying dormant within David's spirit was a seed thought for the future. Could education be made available to the masses through the use of technology? Could the barriers of time and space be removed so that all persons—regardless of their schedules and time constraints—could have the opportunity to obtain a higher education leading to a degree? Some scorned his idea; others were receptive. David's idea germinated into a dream.

After being appointed to a new position, David began the process of nurturing his dream into a vision. He met with a friend and outlined the broad parameters of his idea. He gathered a team of like-minded technology experts and initiated the planning process. And the vision began to materialize: the first Internet interaction course, the first student, the first class, the first five hundred students and, finally, one of the first regionally accredited full degrees offered online.

The development of online education courses parallels the natural progression evident in the phenomenon of the Internet itself. Take a look back. The Internet was preceded by the invention of the PC, which developed from larger, industry-based computers. The computing conveniences we enjoy today came about because someone had a vision. The vision was conceptualized, became reality and changed the world.

DEFINING VISION

What exactly is vision? Bennis and Nanus define it as "a mental image of a possible and desirable future state of the organization."[1]

Vision sets direction and promotes action.

George Barna agrees when referring to ministry-related vision by suggesting that "vision for ministry is a clear mental image of a preferable future imparted by God . . ."[2]

Most broad-based definitions of vision include these key elements:

- Vision defines the future.
- Vision is purpose driven.
- Vision crystallizes creative thought.
- Vision sets direction and promotes action.
- Vision includes dreams.

- Vision uses wisdom from the past.
- Vision reaches for the impossible.
- Vision becomes reality when conceptualized.
- Vision must be communicated.
- Vision must be shared to overcome hindrances.

Vision without technique and execution is blind.

From these definitions and others, vision can be interpreted as imagining and defining the future. Vision brings order out of chaos. Vision without technique and execution is blind.

From Mission Statement to Vision Statement

Vision has many elements in common with a mission statement. Although many organizations use these terms interchangeably, there are important differences. For the purposes of this text, we prefer to see them as related but different concepts.

Simply stated, the mission statement is the purpose for being, the reason for an individual or organization's existence. As the organization's foundation and framework, the mission statement is the structure through which the vision is realized and enabled. In this capacity, whether for an individual or an organization, a mission statement is more enduring.

The mission statement is the organization's purpose for being.

A vision statement is the confident and realistic expectation that the best we can imagine will come into being. It anticipates the attainment of a strategic plan and implements the goals and actions necessary to achieve that plan. A vision based on the fulfillment of goals and plans has a beginning and an end. Once a particular vision is realized, the individual or change team can form a new vision for another compelling opportunity.

An Example

One university defines itself through its mission statement as *"a Christ-centered academic community committed to changing the world by developing students in character, scholarship and leadership."* This mission statement embodies the university's reason for being. It serves both as a filter for decision making and change within the university, and the enabler of the university's goals and vision. The vision statement states that this university *"will prepare each student to become a world changer. We will accomplish this by drawing students into an integrated experience of intellectual challenge, spiritual growth, and leadership development. Thus we will*

- *call students to Christian character,*
- *expect academic excellence,*
- *equip them for success in their vocations,*
- *mentor them in leadership,*
- *prepare them for service."*[3]

By comparing the university's mission and vision statements, one can begin to see the differences between the two. The vision statement grows out of the mission statement. It becomes the confident expectation of what must be done to fulfill the mission statement.

Questions to Ask

When determining what comprises a personal vision, we usually ask questions such as these:

- What do I want for my life over the next two, five, ten or twenty years?
- What are my core values?
- What is my life purpose?
- How can I use my core competencies to add value to others?
- What can I change to make my world a better place?
- How can I impact the future?
- What cause or societal problem am I passionate about?

Vision Grows out of Mission and Core Values

Developing a vision statement involves looking at your mission and core values. Both the mission statement and core values must be used to steer the vision process; in fact, a vision is only as successful as the mission and core values upon which it is built. Core values are such an ingrained part of our thought processes and exert such a powerful influence over our decisions that most of us cannot move beyond the perimeters they set.

Core values are ideals that guide personal or institutional choices.

What are core values and why are they so significant? Core values are usually thought of as the ideals that guide personal or institutional choices and actions. These ideals are the most important aspects of personal or organizational character. They prompt us to ask these questions:

- What do I really believe are the most important principles governing life?
- What values ground me?
- What will I not compromise?

Examples of societal core values include

- belief in the dignity of life,
- respect for one another's religious views,
- integrity in all situations,
- valuing and appreciating others.

Core values are the heart of a person or organization. For example, one academic institution tests its vision statement according to the following core values:

- Christ-likeness—a primary value
- Commitment
- Learning
- Serving
- Stewardship[4]

Brainstorming a Vision

In any brainstorming session, core values are the filter through which vision development must pass. No matter what an individual or an organization's public rhetoric might suggest, core values are what govern daily life. An employee who does not know and understand the core values of an organization is at a major disadvantage. On the other hand, employees who understand the vision and values of the institution for which they work are more likely to succeed in making the contribution expected of them. In short, a personal or organizational vision always must be tested against or framed by its established core values.

MAKING IT PERSONAL:
Confronting Compromise

This kind of commitment can be challenging. After completing its strategic plan, one organization identified certain core values as inviolable—these were never to be compromised. Several years later the organization faced a difficult situation that directly pitted its core values against the profitability of the company. If the company compromised its core values, it would lose the chance to participate in contract bidding. After many hours of discussing the positive and negative sides of the issue, the company decided to hold to its core values. The short-term losses seemed enormous but after a few months, sales and overall profits increased. The company realized it had made the right decision. If the company had compromised its core values, the short-term gains eventually could have led to huge long-term losses and security compromises.

Rarely does a person or organization compromise core values without long-term damage.

The wisdom in this example is clearly evident: rarely does a person or organization compromise core values without long-term damage. As you become world changers, our challenge to you is to develop your list of core values and never compromise them. Core values are the key to guiding vision.

MAKING IT PERSONAL:
When Preparation Meets Opportunity

Identifying core values became instrumental in turning one assistant coach's life around. At an "Achieving Your Potential Seminar" in Dallas, Texas, Leon and the other participants were asked to complete a self-assessment. During lunch, Leon shared with the seminar leader that he was dispirited, felt boxed in and had a difficult time generating excitement about his job as an assistant football coach in an inner city high school. The seminar leader asked Leon if he had written a personal mission statement and professional growth goals. When Leon answered no, the leader said, "Leon, you are in the right place at the right time!"

Promotion was the result of preparation meeting opportunity.

That afternoon Leon and the other seminar participants made a list of twenty things they wanted to accomplish in life. They then wrote four to five core values that reflected who they were and how these core values related to what they wanted to accomplish. Next they wrote their life mission statements and developed two life-balance goals, including five or more action steps for each goal. At the end of the seminar, Leon shared his mission statement with the seminar participants: "My life mission is to be faithful in whatever position I have in order that I can get all of my talents into action for the benefit of the organization, those I coach, and my own sense of fulfillment. My core values are: integrity, unity, loyalty, dedication, and hard work."

Leon went back to his coaching position with renewed vision, a positive attitude and a fighting determination to accomplish his professional growth goals. Within two months a tragedy involving the coaching staff resulted in Leon's promotion to the head coaching position for the remainder of the season. The school administration had observed the change in Leon's attitude, work ethic and performance. Because he was passionately pursuing his mission and working on his two professional growth goals, Leon was ready for his new challenge. Promotion was the result of preparation meeting opportunity.

Vision—Reaching for the Stars

As we saw in the Change Model (Figure 1.2, chapter 1), vision involves imagination. Imagination is a word that reminds us of childhood. Lying on the ground watching the clouds float by, you might have dreamed of going to the moon or becoming President. And that is exactly the kind of thinking you must do in order to change your world. Vision is reaching for the moon and holding it in your hand! Well, maybe that metaphor is a bit exaggerated, but the illustration is valid. When it comes to imagining the best for your world, creative genius must be harnessed by nothing less than goodness. When used correctly, imagination is a powerful gift for good.

Vision is reaching for the moon and holding it in your hand!

What's the best you can imagine for your organization? Can you

111

imagine doing the best work of your life every day of your life? How often do you allow your imagination to unleash its creative potential? Imagination rises from a spirit of hope and faith.

As we have already pointed out, organizations in the world today are in critical need of vision and the change agents who possess such vision. Visionaries are needed to change what is seen and envision what is unseen. This kind of creative vision convicts, inspires and enables people in their institutions to attain peak performance and achieve extraordinary goals. We cannot overemphasize the importance of establishing a vision for your life.

Take a moment and think, "What would I do if I had ten million dollars? What changes would I make?" Chances are that you could make some of those changes even *without* having ten million dollars. What would you really like to do, be or become in life? What would you like to change?

At the moment that you begin to ponder these questions, you begin to develop vision.

CONCEPTUALIZING THE VISION

As you begin the process of vision planning, you must understand that it is critical to write down your vision. Visionaries write, publish, and enthusiastically communicate the vision of the organization, project or mission. This can be traced back to biblical times when Habakkuk wrote,

Visionaries write, publish, and enthusiastically communicate the vision.

"Then the Lord told me: 'I will give you my message in the form of a vision. Write it clearly enough to be read at a glance'" (Habakkuk 2:2 CEV).

Great organizations have been birthed by creative imagination. What is your organization's vision? Will it benefit others? Is it clearly written? Is it published and frequently communicated to all stakeholder audiences? Is it future-oriented? Does it bring the future into the present?

Study these questions. They serve as criteria through which to evaluate your vision. Perhaps these questions will enable you to strengthen and revive your vision. Certainly, these questions will help you to write the vision for a new venture or the restructuring of your personal life or organization.

Write It

In writing a vision statement, you are on your way to *conceptualizing* your vision. Remember these important steps:

1. Find a quiet place to reflect on your life.
2. Ask yourself some key questions and write down your answers.
   a. What needs to change in my life? In my work? My society? My world?
   b. What would I do differently if I had ten million dollars?
   c. What would I really like to be remembered for in life?
   d. What do I really value (core values)? Am I devoting myself to what I value?
   e. If I could change my world, what would I change?
3. Choose one area and write how you might go about implementing change.
4. Share your ideas with a friend/colleague.
5. Start thinking about setting goals to accomplish the vision.

Communicate It

Writing the vision statement brings the future into the present. The next step is to communicate the vision. As it is communicated, it will give purpose, set direction, build hope and energize the people around you to have a sense of pride and stakeholder ownership. It will provide direction by raising the standard and setting the course.

> *Writing the vision statement brings the future into the present.*

Institutionalizing the vision is far more than writing it down. The leader has to have a passion for incorporating the vision into the institution or organization, then taking it from its present status to its intended purpose. Having experience in both the educational and corporate worlds, co-author Larry Lindsay puts it this way: "Whatever my work involved, I found it absolutely imperative to clearly communicate and institutionalize the vision. It enables us to see where we are going. The vision mobilizes and energizes people. It promotes collaborative creativity and continuous improvement."

To enable leaders to institutionalize the vision for an organization, he offers this outline:

1. Engage a guiding coalition of several colleagues to write the vision and overarching goals.

2. Utilize a vision team to help you introduce and ratify the shared vision to the staff or employees.

3. Keep the vision and overarching goals before school/ community audiences (i.e., board, staff, students/ customers, suppliers, institutions, networks). Publish it in:

a. bylaws

b. handbooks

c. brochures

d. rooms and offices

e. meeting agendas

f. related literature

g. planners

4. Look to the vision as a filter in conferences, professional development and decision-making meetings.

5. Create an ongoing dialogue of the vision.

6. Celebrate progress toward institutionalizing the vision.

Internalize It

Great leaders know they are called to the vision of an institution. They internalize the vision and become the personification of the vision. They fully subscribe to the vision and have the ability to enroll others in the beliefs, ideals and futuristic outcomes of that vision. Their example, exhortation and enthusiastic work toward the vision transmit belief in, commitment to, and unity with the institutional standard of excellence.

Great leaders become the personification of the vision.

For you the task is clear. On any level—personal or organizational—you must develop your vision, for it is the springboard to purpose, meaning, consistency and excellence.

MAKING IT PERSONAL:
Creating a New Image

When Larry Lindsay was appointed superintendent of a Christian preparatory school in Dallas, Texas, the school board had already decided to make it an *accredited* school. They were in the process of changing the school's name, image, mission and outreach when Larry arrived.

On any level—personal or organizational—you must develop your vision.

The new superintendent's first step was to develop a shared vision. He wanted to accomplish several goals in the transition: create a new image for the school; gain accreditation; raise the standard of excellence in Christian schools across the nation; open up enrollment to families from other evangelical churches in the area; establish an outstanding college-preparatory faculty; and accomplish world-class results.

Given this clear-cut vision for the school, a change facilitation team crafted a new mission statement and began to communicate it to such school/community audiences as the board, faculty, staff, parents, students and prospective families. The new mission statement said this:

The primary mission of the Academy is to become an educational image-bearer for Christ: a model of excellence lighting the pathway for students, faculty, parents, and to be a prototype of Christian preparatory schools across America.

Included in the mission is the standard of excellence in Christian education. This Academy is a K-12 educational institution maintaining high standards spiritually and academically with the purpose of glorifying God and His Son, Jesus Christ. The faculty and administration are committed to teach youth who they are in Christ with Spirit-taught curriculum integrated with pertinent biblical truths.

Graduates will master spiritual truths and academic knowledge leading to success in relation to God, to people, and the world.

Upon hearing of the new mission statement, a successful and prosperous businessman scheduled a meeting with the new leadership team. His bottom-line questions were: "If I keep my children in this academy, can they be accepted—possibly on scholarship—to schools such as Harvard or Southern Methodist University? Will they have the educational foundation, qualifications, and Scholastic Aptitude Test (SAT) scores to get into and graduate from an outstanding university?"

At that time in the first nine years of the school's history, only two students had ever graduated from college. Few graduates were even going to college. SAT scores averaged about 850, with the highest at about 1080. The school was not accredited and the co-curricular performances of music and athletics were mediocre. But there was a God-inspired vision. The vision saw the school

1. attaining high SAT scores;
2. having the best faculty in America;
3. sending 90 percent of its graduates to college with scholarships or financial assistance;
4. having a strong spiritual foundation with college-prep honors courses;

5. winning state championships in athletics and academics;

6. being accredited;

7. being one of the top Christian prep schools in America.

Without blinking at the businessman's questions, the superintendent responded: "Yes, your children will be well prepared and able to be admitted to any university they choose."

The vision had been declared boldly. Now the team had to produce results. Team Leader Larry did qualify the team's assertions. "It's going to take some time," he said. "It won't happen overnight. But our goal is for all graduates to get into universities of their choice on scholarships or with financial help. The students will also grow in the grace and knowledge of Jesus Christ while taking a rigorous and cooperatively competitive college preparatory course of studies."

On that spring day the futuristic vision was spoken in the present. That vision became reality. The businessman's son and daughter later graduated with honors from the academy. Accepted at the universities of their choice, they could have been accepted at Harvard if they had applied. The son subsequently earned his M.A. in accounting and the daughter graduated from Texas A & M University. Both are leading fulfilling careers in the business world.

Subsequent graduates have been admitted to the top schools in the nation, including West Point, Princeton University, Texas A & M University, the University of Texas, Texas Christian University, Southern Methodist University, Baylor University, the University of Michigan, and Wheaton College. What began as a vision for this academy, an imagined goal of becoming one of the top prep schools in America, became reality.[5]

From Vision to Strategy

Great personal achievers have clearly stated vision statements. These statements are well written, easily understood and broadly communicated. They serve as a guide for decisions.

Great personal achievers have clearly stated vision statements.

As you study your organization's vision, determine if it is effectively published and broadly communicated. Ask yourself if it contradicts or supports your personal mission statement. Does it inspire people to action and serve as a filter for decision making? Perhaps it needs revision. If your organization does not have a vision statement, you may be the one to approach the subject.

The only way to change your world effectively is to identify a key area that you are passionate about and suggest a plan to implement change. Remember that world changers are vision planners.

In his best-selling book, *The 21 Irrefutable Laws of Leadership,* John Maxwell writes about the Law of Buy-In. He says, "People buy into the leader, then the vision."[6] Once the leader begins to clearly see a vision and to mobilize a guiding coalition to shape, crystallize and own the vision, a synergy of collective intelligence is then ready to run with the vision. That is the time to write the goals and action steps to bring the vision into reality.

Questions to Ponder

At the beginning of this chapter we asked you to measure your vision against your core values. As you begin to develop your strategic plan, ask yourself these questions:

What's Important Now? – Lou Holtz

What one issue would I most like to change about my world/my organization? What's important now?

_____

_____

_____

_____

_____

_____

What core values undergird this proposed change?

_____

_____

_____

_____

_____

Who will benefit from the change? Who's important now?

_____

_____

_____

_____

_____

_____

With whom should I share my vision?

_____

_____

_____

_____

_____

_____

How would I word my initial vision statement?

_____

_____

_____

_____

_____

What is the best I can imagine for this project (i.e., changing the seen and shaping the unseen)?

_____

_____

_____

_____

Harness the power

_____

of creative imagination.

_____

> *WIN WIN NOW*
>
> *What's Important Now?*
>
> *Who's Important Now?*
>
> *– Lou Holtz & Larry Lindsay[7]*

What passions do I feel at the thought of the vision becoming reality?

_____

_____

_____

_____

_____

_____

_____

_____

Endnotes

1. Bennis and Nanus, *Leaders*, 89.
2. George Barna, *Without a Vision, the People Perish: A Barna Report* (Glendale, CA: Barna Research Group Ltd., 1991), 29.
3. Vision and mission statements are those of Indiana Wesleyan University, Marion, Indiana.
4. Ibid.
5. No longer affiliated with this academy, Larry reports that it has undergone organizational changes and recently merged with another institution.
6. John Maxwell, *The 21 Irrefutable Laws of Leadership* (Nashville: Thomas Nelson, 1998), 143.
7. Co-author Larry Lindsay created "Win Win Now" by adapting his "Who's Important Now" and Lou Holtz's "What's Important Now" from a March 2002 presentation in Atlanta.

Learning Activities—Chapter 5

Real change leaders harness the inner power of creative imagination as they seek to be the best they can be for the world.

1. Now that you have a mission statement (i.e., personal constitution) you need to reach a vision of significance for the next three–five years. Look at page 113 in the book. Answer questions "a" through "e" and engage in thinking for the clear vision you want to accomplish over the next three–five years.

2. Think about the Lou Holtz question, "What's Important Now?" Then thoughtfully engage in successful thinking (i.e., practical, creative, analytical, and reflective thinking) as you answer the six leading change questions (pp. 120-122). Put the questions and your thoughtful responses in your Leading Change Journal. This is a "win-win" ritual that will help you crystallize a clear and compelling vision of what you want to accomplish (i.e., know, be, do, or have) over the short term.

3. As you engage in thinking for constructive change, you will begin to crystallize a vision that will result in collaborative and coordinated actions aimed at being an agent of change and significant person in your sphere of influence. Study your mission statement, values, indicators of personal mastery, "vision statement", and two SMART goals. In what ways does your emerging strategic plan inspire you to know, be, do, and accomplish more?

∞ Notes & Ideas ∞

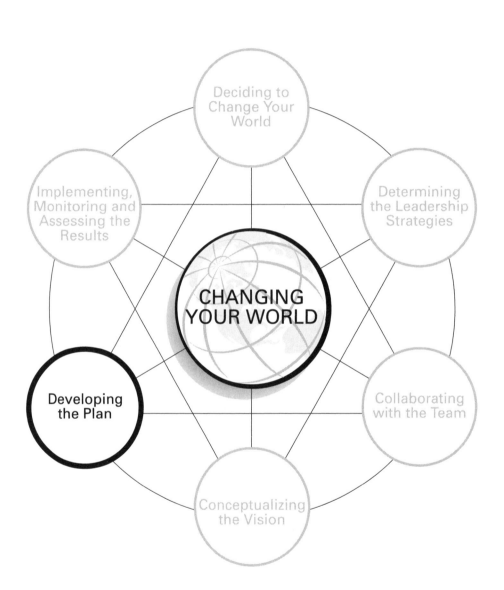

Deciding to Change Your World

Determining the Leadership Strategies

Implementing, Monitoring and Assessing the Results

CHANGING YOUR WORLD

Collaborating with the Team

Developing the Plan

Conceptualizing the Vision

6

PLOTTING THE COURSE
Developing a Strategic Plan

> *"Never doubt that a small group of thoughtful,
> committed people can change the world;
> indeed it is the only thing that ever has."* [1]
>
> ~ *Margaret Mead*

Crystallizing the Vision

Henry Moore noted, "The secret of life is to have a task, something you devote your entire life to, something you bring everything to, every minute of the day for your whole life."[2] Perhaps you have already begun that task or assignment and wish more systematically and purposefully to devote time to renew or create a strategic plan that will ensure fulfillment of that mission. Or perhaps you have identified a life-changing or world-changing project—one that will lead to the improvement of people, programs, or organizations—and now need to devote quality time for strategic planning.

"The future is not some place we are going, but one we create," John Schaar said. "The paths are not found, but made, and the activity of making them changes both the maker and the destination."[3] This is reflected in Gandhi's comment, "We must be the change we wish to see in the world."[4]

> *We must be the change we wish to see in the world.*

In this chapter, utilizing analysis and decision making, you will begin to develop a strategic plan that will enable you to collaborate with others in creating productive change in the workplace, community, church or families within your sphere of influence. Unless we venture to create productive change, we are unable to project ourselves as agents of change. And the best way to change our world is strategically to influence teams of empowered and equipped people who will create productive change.

It Takes Two or More—Teaming

As we have seen in previous chapters, when you move from personal mastery to becoming an agent of change on behalf of others, you move into the sphere of interpersonal and organizational influence. Before you identify people, issues or programs that you believe need to be changed, you must understand that since others are part of the issues, they must be part of the strategic planning for transformation. Even though you see a need to initiate change, it is important that others join with you in the process.

Your help, inspired idea or services must be accepted, trusted and owned by others before you truly can be an agent of change. Therefore, it is vital that you identify a partner or a change facilitation team to work with you on any life-changing or workplace-changing project.

MAKING IT PERSONAL:
Teamwork within a Family Framework

Phil and Mary Lou loved kids. The parents of two boys, they had a passion to help in the nursery of a large church in Dallas. While working in the nursery, they met a teenage girl whose parents had divorced. Her mother, father and other family members were in no position to raise her. So Phil and Mary Lou decided to take Denise into their home. This compassionate couple served as agents of change in Denise's life. They provided a happy, healthy home life for Denise. They taught her Judeo-Christian values, a good work ethic and the importance of education in preparation for a better quality of life. They paid for and helped her to earn tuition to go to a Christian preparatory school.

Denise graduated with honors from a rigorous college preparatory course of studies. During her senior year she won the Outstanding Young American scholarship contest for juniors and seniors from high schools throughout the Dallas Metroplex. Phil, Mary Lou and their two sons were world changers in their circle of influence.

The key to this story is not the love, privilege and success that Denise experienced as a result of Phil and Mary Lou's decision to raise her through her junior and senior high school years. The key is that this was a team success. Phil and Mary Lou had to obtain the approval of Denise's family for the living arrangements. Denise had to agree to the arrangements and positively respond to her surrogate parents. It took change facilitation team learning, team building and team playing to produce the desired success. Teamwork was the key to enabling these people to work together toward a common vision.

FIGURE 6.1

Team Learning Cycle

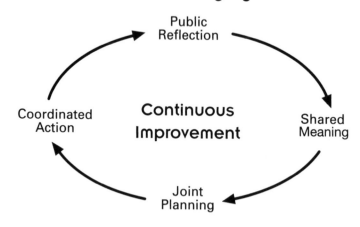

The Team Learning Cycle—A Model for Decision Making

As demonstrated in Denise's story, creatively and cooperatively working with others is essential to realizing a goal, fulfilling a vision and bettering the world. Building and working with a collaborative team enlarges thinking, expands capabilities and increases the impact of the team's success.

Stephanie Spear of Innovation Associates developed a "team learning cycle" for the *Fifth Discipline Fieldbook.*[5] (See Figure 6.1.)

As Figure 6.1 illustrates, team learning is a four-phase process that works effectively with all project-focused teams. Phase one is *public reflection.* The expectation is that the team will engage in open and honest public reflection, sharing concerns or ideas for what needs to be done relative to an issue under consideration. During public reflection, team members need to suspend assumptions, openly listen to what others have to say, and engage in the conversations that will both clarify the issue and crystallize thinking.

In phase two of the Team Learning Cycle, individuals create *shared meaning* regarding the issues and inspired ideas under discussion. During this phase, project team members come to a mutual and meaningful understanding of concerns, ideas and actions.

In phase three, the collaborative project team begins to develop a strategy to close the gap between current reality (i.e., the issue being resolved) and the vision, goals and actions moving the issue to a desired state of affairs. *Joint planning* will lead to a sense of commitment, responsibility and accountability to resolve the issue.

In phase four, the team is ready to combine all of the elements of the first three phases and engage in *coordinated action* to implement, monitor and assess the goals. Through coordinated action the team is able to share the vision, empower broad-based action, and engage in accomplishing the goals for the project.

Working as a team toward a common goal requires wise management of data, collective problem solving and a shared vision that results in a decision with the best interest of the stakeholders in mind. Certain team skills must interface effectively with the vision concepts. Four pivotal interactive skills that must be practiced in analysis and decision making are inquiry, dialogue, collaboration, and reflection. Practiced in all phases of the team learning cycle, these processes and skills will provide the fundamentals you must skillfully practice in selecting and building the change facilitation team for its first change project. It is at this stage that we move from "me thinking" to "we thinking." It is important for you to share your vision for the project broadly enough so that your team members all develop a sense of ownership and shared vision.

Creating Productive Change

Total Leaders discusses the critical components of the strategic design process for creating and facilitating productive change.[6] The authors identify five pillars and statements for team understanding and shared meaning:

1. Purpose   It has meaning for everyone on the team.

2. Vision   It's clear and exciting for everyone on the team.

3. Ownership   Everyone wants to be part of the opportunity.

4. Capacity   We can and we will get the project done well.

5. Support   Our agent of change is helping us.

The strategic design process pays great dividends in the world of business. It can be used effectively for any organizational change or innovation. As we suggested earlier, the process of strategic planning proposed for your world-changing project involves the following steps:

- Identifying a compelling opportunity or a problem to solve
- Deciding to pursue the opportunity or tackle the problem
- Identifying a like-minded change facilitation team
- Encouraging team commitment and team building
- Adopting a model to move the team from analysis, to decision making, to implementation, to monitoring, to evaluation

It is both challenging and invigorating to seize the opportunity to create productive change in a group or organization. The passionate pursuit of creating the productive change becomes a way of life for the team if the team is to successfully bring about the intended results.

Engaging in Productive Change

As you begin to take positive action toward making your world a better place, it is important to be as systematic as possible. Concentrated thoughts, creative ideas and synergistic actions will produce intended results. To better direct team efforts toward the accomplishment of collective goals, we propose the PISCO model.

The PISCO Model

The PISCO model (Figure 6.2) is an analysis and decision-making/problem-solving model offered as a means of maintaining a team-learning, systematic approach to achieving shared goals.

FIGURE 6.2

Problem-Solving Model (PISCO)

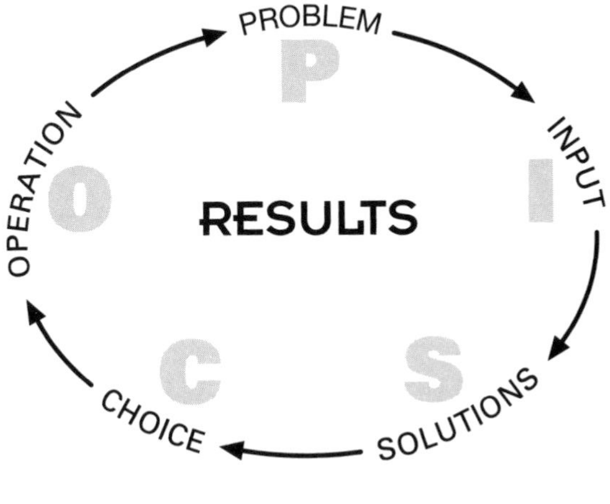

Edward de Bono[7] developed this problem-solving acronym (PISCO) that enables an individual or team to deal with complex problems or innovation opportunities in a simple and practical manner.

For the purposes of this book, a *problem* is defined as something that must be resolved to make things better in your world. And an *opportunity* is defined as an inspired idea or compelling reason to make something better in your circle of influence. We have adapted de Bono's PISCO problem-solving model to help you and your team in developing your strategic plan.

PROBLEM (P)

What is the problem or critical need for which you are resolving a problem or creating an opportunity? Clearly define your problem or opportunity. Then write a clear and concise problem or opportunity statement for the critical need or compelling idea. Focus points should include:

1. **Specificity**

   As you describe the problem for your analysis and decision making, answer who, what, when, where, why and how questions.

2. **Motive**

   The ethical filter should be, "Is our motive pure—the right thing to do—and in the best interest of those involved?"

3. **Problem or Opportunity Statement**

   A problem statement explains how to fix, improve or grow in

the area of need. An opportunity statement expresses how to create, innovate and invent in the area of need.

4. Core Values

What core values should guide the change facilitation team's work in resolving the issues? Values such as integrity, truth, compassion, responsibility and cooperation are examples of core values.

INPUT (I)

In finding a viable solution for your problem or opportunity, it is vital to gather all the need-to-know information bearing on the issue. Be sure to wisely manage the facts in the analysis and decision-making actions. Focus points should include:

1. Relevant information

Generate all the relevant need-to-know information regarding data, numbers, causes, surveys, observations and research that must be considered in resolving the problem or creating the opportunity.

2. Obstacles

What obstacles are preventing the team from finding the information it needs?

3. Rewriting

As you analyze the need-to-know information, it is possible that the problem or opportunity statement has taken on a slightly different focus. Since this is a paramount issue, it is good to rewrite this statement in order to bring even greater focus on the root-causal issue. Has your statement taken on a different focus? If so, thoughtfully rewrite the more focused problem or opportunity statement.

SOLUTIONS (S)

As you seek resolution of the problem or study a creative idea for an opportunity, it is important to generate several possible solutions. Given three or four possible solutions, the team should carefully analyze each of the alternatives to ensure that the best possible solution is acted upon. Which alternative solution is the best? Have all the costs been considered in choosing this solution? Is the change facilitation team convinced the best solution will resolve the issue? Focus points should include:

1. **Imagination**

    Now is the time to think creatively and positively about the best possible solutions. It is time to really harness the power of the group's imagination. What solutions will produce fundamental, optimal change? How can you make the change work?

2. **SWOT analysis**

    In analyzing the alternative solutions, the team should consider the strengths, weaknesses, opportunities and threats (SWOT) of each proposed solution. One of the solutions should emerge as the best and most feasible.

CHOICE (C)

Given the analysis and evaluation of the alternative solutions, what is the best way to make the constructive change? Select the best alternative or a blend of the three most feasible alternatives as your choice (decision). Rewrite the choice statement clearly and concisely. Focus points should include:

1. **Choice Statement**

   The change facilitation team should write this in clear, concise language. Briefly support why you believe this choice is the best possible decision. What are the anticipated benefits?

2. **Vision**

   What is the best the team can imagine for the problem or opportunity? The change facilitation team should develop a shared vision for the project. It is important to use the team's creative imagination at this point to envision the best possible future for the issue.

3. **Goals**

   Write the choice statement as a SMART goal (or goals if needed). Carefully align the goals with the rewritten problem or opportunity statement. This enables the team to be sure it is attending to the compelling needs of the issue.

OPERATION (O)

The operational plan is the critical element for change in an individual, unit or organization. The project team should write a clear and concise plan for the choice. Writing goals and strategic actions crystallizes thoughts and promotes productive action. The next step is to write the choice as an operational goal or goals. Be specific. After writing the goal statements for the choice (decision), the project team should write five or more action steps that will enable the successful implementation and fulfillment of the choice. Once the goals and implementation steps are developed, it is necessary to design processes to implement, monitor and measure the operational plan. The team should make the effort to celebrate short-term gains and build on the gains to create more change in the individual, unit or organization. Focus points should include:

1. **Five or more implementation/action steps**

    What is the best way to create the change? What must be done? Who is the champion for each part of the strategic plan? Is the responsibility clearly communicated to key stakeholders? Who is responsible for implementing the overall operational (strategic) plan? How can you effectively communicate the change or innovation to all stakeholders? How can you empower broad-based actions such as training, modifying the culture, developing new systems, and so forth, as the change requires the involvement of people beyond the change facilitation team?

2. **Monitoring and Assessing**

    Who is monitoring the plan? How well are you following the plan? What assessment or feedback data do you need to be collecting along the way? Based on the formative assessment data, what course corrections do you need to make?

3. Institutionalizing

How can you create a culture of continuous improvement? How can you be sure there is mutual understanding, a spirit of collaboration and a shared vision among stakeholders? How can you be sure that the systems have been put into place that will sustain the change or innovation? How can you recognize and reward people instrumental in the success of the operational plan?

Lifting the Lid—The Six-Hat Model

Strategic planning requires team members to engage cooperatively in *creative* thinking, *analytical* thinking and *optimistic* thinking. The change facilitation team must diligently build a community of trust, respect and confidence in one another before commencing to move an issue or inspired idea from current reality (i.e., seeing what is) to optimal vision (i.e., seeing the best we can imagine). Recognizing the various talents and capabilities of the team members is implicit in developing an effective strategic plan.

De Bono writes, "Thinking is the ultimate human resource. Yet we can never be satisfied with our most important skill. No matter how good we become, we should always want to be better."[8] His book title, *Six Thinking Hats,* refers to the six thinking hats that enhance the analysis, decision-making, and strategic-planning processes. The six hats provide decision makers a vivid, easy way to visualize and remember the respective roles and attention-directing actions a change team needs to practice during team meetings. We have adapted the meaning and application of the six hats and how they fit into the PISCO model as follows:

1. **White Hat.** The white hat focuses on need-to-know information: facts, numbers, research, personal notes, reports and pertinent data bearing on the issue. White hat thinking is especially useful in the "input" section of the PISCO model.

2. **Red Hat.** The red hat focuses on emotions, feelings and passion. Whether the emotion is anger, fear, frustration and despair, or excitement, compassion, peace and determination, the red hat symbolizes the emotional fuel to resolve the issue or create the opportunity. Red-hat thinking is most useful in the "choice" section. A passionate desire to solve the problems strengthens the commitment to see the project through.

3. **Black Hat.** The black hat causes one to count the costs, to look at the negative or opposing side of the issue. In the analysis process, one should look at an issue inside out and upside down to be sure there are no hidden consequences that might cause a solution to flounder. Visionaries tend to leap before they look. For them it is vital to have team members that will look at every angle of the issue before making a decision to "go." Black-hat thinking is useful in the "solutions" section of PISCO thinking.

4. **Yellow Hat.** The yellow hat represents the sunny side of the issue. No negative thinking is allowed when wearing the yellow hat. This hat represents the optimistic, hopeful and positive viewpoints of the team as members analyze the issue. Yellow-hat thinking is a logical,

positive counterbalance of logical, negative black-hat thinking. It also represents the "solutions" section of the PISCO model. What are the positive benefits of each solution and our choice (decision)?

5. **Green Hat.** The green hat represents creativity, growth, productive change and innovation. It is important to wear the green hat and to play that role when brainstorming and looking for exciting, viable solutions or opportunities. The choice and operational plan will grow out of green-hat thinking and strategizing. It represents "operations" in the PISCO model.

6. **Blue Hat.** The blue hat represents facilitation, gate-keeping and synthesis of the team's ideas and opinions. As such, it can be seen as reflecting the "purpose" of the PISCO model. The facilitator of the team meetings will wear the blue hat.

Employing six-hat thinking and acting in the communication process will build upon the strengths of the change facilitation team members and enhance PISCO problem solving. For example, the team facilitator (blue hat) might say, "Let's all put on our green hats and brainstorm a number of possible solutions." Or she could say, "It appears we have come upon a viable solution. Let's put on our black hats and see if there is anything that might cause this solution to go south."

By incorporating strategic, analytical, creative and optimistic thinking, the six-hat model lifts the lid and promotes imaginative, "out-of-box" thinking. De Bono notes five purposes to six-hat thinking (lateral thinking):[9]

1. **Role playing**: enables team members to be aware of the focus of their collaborative efforts during lateral thinking. For example, the team facilitator may say, "Let's put on our green hats and do some out-of-the-box creative generation of three or four viable solutions for our issue."

2. **Attention directing**: enables the team members to focus their attention during lateral thinking on feelings (red hat), facts (white hat), logical positives (yellow hat), logical negatives (black hat), and so forth. The purpose of attention directing is to narrow the focus of the collaborative effort on the specific phase of the analysis and decision making that is taking place in the team in order to come up with the best possible solution.

3. **Convenience**: the six thinking hats (i.e., lateral thinking processes) enable the team to move quickly from one phase of lateral thinking to another; that is, to move from creative green-hat thinking to analytical yellow-, black-, and red-hat thinking in making the best decision possible.

4. **Possible basis in brain chemistry** (extrapolation): the lateral thinking processes enable the team to engage both the right and left hemispheres of the brain. As a result, the holistic and lateral-thinking processes energize the team members and enable them to fully utilize their logic and reasoning capabilities, while engaging their imaginative and intuitive skills to seek the best possible solution.

5. **Rules of the game** (rules of team thinking during a meeting): the lateral-thinking process enables all of the team members to work together collegially in focusing their unified efforts on finding the best answer to a perplexing question or the best solution to a major problem.

Your priority issue might be mentoring a friend or colleague who is dealing with a serious issue in one or more of life's domains. Or, it could be helping to improve employee morale in a small business. It might be helping a local service organization attack alcohol and drug abuse problems in the community. Each of these issues can be approached with six-hat thinking and the PISCO problem-solving model. As you can see, the PISCO model will work for problem solving, conflict resolution and project decision making.

The Challenge

You have had time for reflective thought about how you might make a greater difference in your world. You have shown a desire to step beyond yourself, to move from self to service, from life-balance to life-service. You also have been introduced to some skills, models and principles for bringing about constructive change in your circle of influence. Your challenge

Simply stated, agents of change are winners who enthusiastically respond to the challenge of creating a better world.

now is to make a corresponding action of commitment to some person, group or organization—an action that will positively influence your world.

143

As you begin a change project, consider Robert Schuller's words: "I've learned one important thing about living. I can do anything I think I can—but I can't do anything alone. No one can go it alone. Create your own team!"[10]

Develop your team, create your vision, conduct some analysis and decision making, write your strategic plan and be astounded at the excitement you will generate as the intended results materialize. And don't forget to look at yourself and your mission as Dennis Waitley might: "Winners can tell you where they are going, what they plan to do along the way and who will be sharing the adventure with them."[11]

Simply stated, agents of change are winners who enthusiastically respond to the challenge of creating a better world. They really believe they can somehow make things better.

Endnotes

1. As quoted in *Celebrating Excellence: Quality, Service, Teamwork, and the Quest for Excellence* (Lombard, IL: Celebrating Excellence Publishing Company, 1992), 58.

2. Bob Buford, *Game Plan: Winning Strategies for the Second Half of Your Life* (Grand Rapids: Zondervan Publishing House, 1997), 99.

3. Ibid., 55.

4. As quoted in *Half Time* by Bob Buford, 35.

5. *The Fifth Discipline Fieldbook*, 60.

6. Charles J. Schwann and others, *Total Leaders: Applying the Best Future-Focused Change Strategies to Education* (AASA Distribution Center, 1998), 22-23.

7. Edward de Bono, *Six Thinking Hats* (Boston: Little, Brown and Company, 1985), 31-32.

8. Ibid., 2.

9. Ibid, 29-30.

10. *Celebrating Excellence*, 70.

11. Ibid., 68.

Learning Activities—Chapter 6

Significant win-win people strategically plan their course from the inspiration of their mission, vision, and goals. And when they do, success and significance in life follows.

1. Real change leaders must plan to achieve the vision in their heart, prepare to achieve the vision, expect to achieve the vision, and celebrate achieving the vision. You have created a strategic vision for Being the Best for the World, Inc. You have a mission statement, core values, indicators of personal mastery, a vision statement, and two SMART goals. Carefully review your strategic plan and be sure you have built in the action steps (tactics) that will start you on the Leading Change in Your World journey that will enable you to be the best you can be for the world.

2. In what ways will your strategic plan enable you to do things better?

3. Complete the phrase, "It would be amazing if . . ."

∽ Notes & Ideas ∽

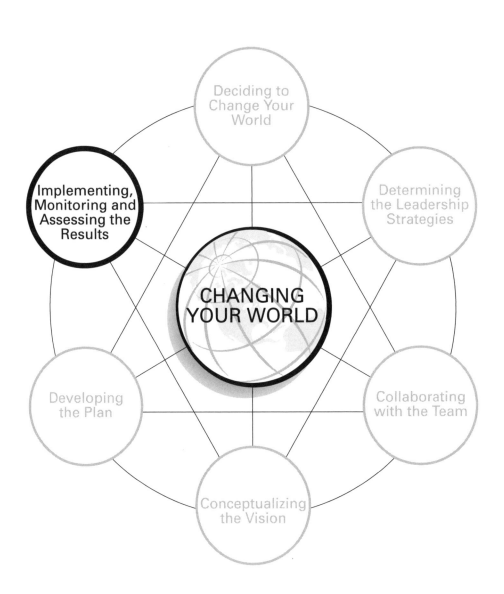

Deciding to Change Your World

Determining the Leadership Strategies

Implementing, Monitoring and Assessing the Results

CHANGING YOUR WORLD

Collaborating with the Team

Developing the Plan

Conceptualizing the Vision

7

MAKING IT WORK
Implementing, Monitoring and Assessing the Intended Results

*"Even if you're on the right track,
you'll get run over if you just sit there." [1]*

∽ *Will Rogers*

Fuel for the Fire

There are four steps to accomplishment:

1. **PLAN** purposefully.
2. **PREPARE** thoroughly.
3. **PROCEED** carefully.
4. **PURSUE** vigorously.[2]

Whether implementing change or renewal, these four steps signal a need for high moral purpose. Optimistic action based on these steps will make the difference between "we're glad we did" and "we wish we had." Dreaming about a world-changing project before implementing it is the normal course. But continuing to dream about the project when we should be implementing it is off course.

Do not confuse activity with accomplishment.

Tragically, it is at the point of implementation that many strategic plans for productive change fail. They fail because they never get successfully implemented, monitored and assessed during the operational stages of the project. As you contemplate the strategic plan you have so carefully devised and organized, it is time to begin a passionate, persistent pursuit toward accomplishing your intended results. Tenacity, persistence, perseverance and a fighting determination to succeed are the fuels that will energize and sustain your team efforts.

The Determination to Change—Implementation

At this point in the change process you have:

1. identified an area of needed change;
2. assembled your team, including the leadership;
3. established a shared vision; and
4. developed a strategic plan to solve a problem or create an opportunity.

The challenge now is to implement the project effectively. To put it another way, your team thus far has taken time to think it, see it, believe it, plan it, ink it and communicate it.

Now it is time to begin it, do it, correct it, complete it, celebrate it and renew it!

The Challenge of Implementing

Once a strategic plan has been determined, it must be implemented into the daily work of the individual, group or organization. The focus changes from what is *hoped for or intended to what gets done.* Benjamin Franklin wrote, "Well done is better than well said."[3] An effective change project—one that produces intended results that can be "operationalized" (i.e., internalized as habit or institutionalized into the culture and organizational systems) within an individual, group or organization—starts with a compelling need and continues throughout the project.

It is one thing to say you intend to do something and it is quite another to actually do it. Eddie Rickenbacker said, "I can give you a six-word formula for success: Think things through—then follow through."[4] However, it is at the stage of implementation that the most difficult work begins. This is the follow-through stage in the change process. The core values, vision, mission, strategic goals and action steps must be clearly understood and shared among all stakeholders. The change facilitation team must empower broad-based actions throughout the team, department or organization. The team will have to overcome resistance and obstacles every step of the way. It is at the stage of implementation that the little things done right—attention to detail—will make a big difference toward producing the intended results.

Commit to Continuous Improvement

One of the most difficult aspects of the implementation process involves getting the right mindset to change a given area. In *See You at the Top*, Zig Ziglar coaches people to think and say, "I'm Super Good, but I'll Get Better!"[5] That is the mindset for a commitment to continuous improvement. The notion of *good-better-best* is vital for all people living in the twenty-first century because continuous improvement is tantamount to productive and enduring change.

The little things done right—attention to detail—will make a big difference toward producing the intended results.

Peter Senge defines learning organizations as "organizations where people continually expand their capacity to create the results they truly desire, where new and expansive patterns of thinking are nurtured, where collective aspiration is set free and where people are continually learning how to learn together."[6]

It is accepted that ours is the "information age." The quest for knowledge occupies people at every level. People seek knowledge for life-balance, to increase work skills and efficiency, to gain a competitive edge. Knowledge is freely accessible and constantly expanding. Therefore, people who wish to produce quality workmanship on the job and who seek a healthy quality of life will need to make an ongoing commitment to continuous improvement. Four things are necessary as you seek to master this stage of commitment:

1. **Develop the habit of self-directed learning.** Learn at home, in the car while driving, at the workplace or through

formal seminars and courses. Keep up with the fact and knowledge base for your profession, and the skills required to make a worthwhile life.

2. **Be determined to increase your value in the workplace and every domain of your circle of influence.** Be one that others seek out for help or counsel.

3. **Regularly reflect upon what you have learned and count the benefits.** Keep a learning journal to help you assess your results and sense of contribution toward making things better.

4. **Teach someone else something.** To have taught is to have learned better. To have helped an individual or a group learn something useful is to have begun the process of changing your world.

Walt Disney said, "All our dreams can come true—if we have the courage to pursue them."[7] Our emerging dream is to be a world changer. It begins with personal change and moves outward to helping others make a greater difference in their lives and their circles of influence.

Monitor the Change Process

The change facilitation team is active in developing a shared vision, writing the strategic plan and identifying the initial obstacles that must be overcome. Team members also should champion the change project, communicate the

Together
Everyone
Accomplishes
Miracles

vision and model the desired attitude and behavior of all involved in the process. As the guiding coalition of the change project, they must communicate clearly, inspire creativity and encourage appropriate risk taking and decision making to ensure results-oriented action. They also must be vigilant in dealing with unanticipated problems, risks and uncertainties. This calls for continuous monitoring. The change facilitation team can practice effective monitoring in two ways:

1. **Conduct Regular Team Meetings and Accountability Coaching Sessions**

   The change facilitation team continuously needs to monitor its progress, facilitate necessary training and modify systems and practices that may hinder the attainment of intended results. A commitment to the mission and an attitude of vigilance in managing the change process is imperative. Communicating, celebrating small victories and sharing success vignettes among all employees and stakeholders is an important aspect of meetings and coaching sessions.

2. **Engage in Continuous Team Learning**

   The change facilitation team will enable all involved in the change process to engage in public reflection, shared meaning and goal-oriented actions. Team members regularly need to engage in conversation in order to identify the driving and restraining forces and to sense the pulse of those affected by change. The team should focus on questions such as these:

   a. What are people involved in the change processes thinking?

b. How are people involved in the change feeling?

c. What is working well?

d. What needs to be done differently?

e. What feedback needs to be acted upon to ensure the desired outcome of the project?

It is in the process of reflective thinking and assessment that people are able to make the cause-and-effect connections to the change strategies. This feedback information enables the change facilitation team to make the course corrections that will produce the intended results and to identify short-term successes that help to operationalize (institutionalize) the change within the culture.

Assess the Intended Results: Build the Framework

One of the most important aspects of any individual or organization's success involves the assessment of goals.

- Are the goals being met?
- Does assessment result in continuous improvement?
- Are there *formative* (review of data related to goals in the beginning or middle of the project) and *summative* (end-of-goal data review) assessment times built into the process of review?
- Is there a plan to celebrate incremental progress toward the desired end?
- Are success stories (relative to benefits accruing from teamwork and project impact) being shared not only with team members but outside as well?

In assessing its processes and overall quality, one educational organization used a systems-based approach to the administration and operation of educational programming and services. Through a series of division-wide meetings, the employees worked through a process of self-education and planning. This began with a thorough review of the assessment literature and the organization's history.

Based on this review, the organization settled on an assessment model outlined by James O. Nichols. His very useful handbook, *A Practitioner's Handbook for Institutional Effectiveness and Student Outcomes Assessment Implementation,* became the primary resource guiding the development of the division's assessment framework.

The Critical Elements of the Assessment Framework

Nichols outlines the following major components of an assessment framework in what he calls "the critical elements of the Institutional Effectiveness Paradigm"[8]:

1. Establishment of an expanded statement of institutional purpose

2. Identification of intended educational (instructional), research, and service outcomes/administrative objectives

3. Assessment of the extent to which the intended outcomes and objectives are being accomplished

4. Adjustment of the institution's purpose, intended outcomes/objectives, or activities based on assessment findings

Steps to Building the Assessment Framework

Building on this basic model, the above-mentioned educational organization moved forward in building its assessment framework by taking three steps:

1. **Assessment was "institutionalized."** This process included the following elements:
   - **Assessment Meetings.** Departments held monthly assessment planning meetings. Departments conducted an annual "Assessment Day" to review data, summarize findings, draw conclusions, plan institutional adjustments and refocus the process for the coming year. The administration conducted an annual division-wide "Assessment Day" in which departments reported their findings and the division sanctioned institutional adjustments growing out of the previous year's assessment efforts.

   - **Data Collection.** The division developed proposals to upgrade its data collection equipment (computer, scanner and software) to handle increased volume. A person was assigned the responsibility of collecting the data, and budgets were proposed in support of assessment activities.

   - **Reporting.** The Coordinator of Assessment produced an Annual Summary Assessment Report for the division and for the university administration.

   - **Timeline.** The division established a timeline and schedule for the review of its programs.

2. **The administration committed the necessary resources and time to enable the process to function.** In addition to focusing the efforts of the existing faculty and staff on this area, the administration created a new position, granted faculty release time and purchased needed equipment. Just as important, central administrators made assessment a high priority in strategic planning.

3. **The administration, faculty and staff of the division learned how to implement the chosen assessment model by working through the following steps:**

   1. They explored the mission of the division in relationship to the overarching institutional mission. From this process they articulated a set of broad division goals and tied them directly to the mission.

   2. Each department produced a mission statement that tied directly to the overall mission statement.

   3. Each department developed specific objectives tied to their mission statements.

   4. Each department chose instruments by which to measure their stated objectives.

   5. Measurement instruments collected data. Data was then analyzed and conclusions sought.

   6. Departments "closed the loop" by using their assessment data to make institutional adjustments. These changes were approved through normal academic and administrative channels, and budgets were affected accordingly.

"Assessing" the Assessment Framework

After establishing the assessment framework, faculty and administrators were able to focus on the articulation of objectives and the selection of instruments used to measure the achievement of each objective. This work was carried out during the departments' monthly assessment planning meetings. It required months of concerted effort but in the end each department had an assessment plan that articulated goals, objectives, measurement instruments, performance criteria, data collection steps and feedback loops.[9]

Assess the Intended Results: Follow a Model

In Figure 7.1 we present a simple assessment model based on the

FIGURE 7.1

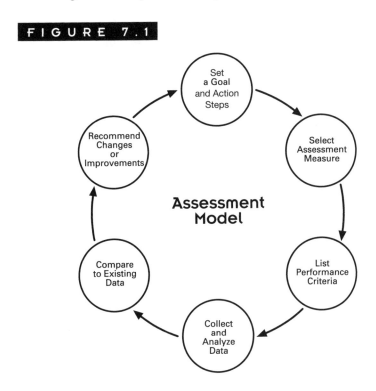

following steps:

1. Set a goal and action steps.

2. Select an assessment measure.

3. List performance criteria.

4. Collect and analyze the data.

5. Compare to existing data.

6. Recommend changes or improvements.

This assessment model illustrates not only how to assess a project, but also how to maintain organizational or individual accountability.

Put It into Practice

Let's use this assessment model in a hypothetical family budget situation.

1. **Set a goal and action steps:** Our family will attain financial stability with 10 percent savings or investment each month.

2. **Select an assessment measure:** We will maintain accurate financial records for one year.

3. **List performance criteria:** Within one year the household will be financially stable with all bills paid on time. An excess of 10 percent will be available each month.

4. **Collect and analyze data:** We will track data from each month's financial records.

5. **Compare new data to existing data:** We will compare data to that of previous years.

6. **Recommend Changes:** After a review of all documents, we will recommend changes for the next year and set new goals.

Assessment Questions

As an organization begins the assessment process, it should ask the following questions:

1. To what extent are we effectively implementing measurable goals of the strategic plan?

2. Are we achieving the intended results?

3. What assessment evidence (both qualitative and quantitative) are we willing to accept that demonstrates we are accomplishing the intended results?

4. How do we measure results?

5. Who is responsible for assimilating the data?

6. How do we analyze and report the data?

MAKING IT PERSONAL: How Do You Measure Success?

It is in the area of assessment and accountability that many projects fail. If sustainable evidence of success cannot be given, failure will result. An example of this is found in the story of Jack, a young and enthusiastic manager who was constantly boasting about the performance of his project team. The company president of the small business happened to hear Jack one day. The president asked him a simple question: "What is your evidence of success?"

Jack was stunned by the question. He asked, "What do you mean when you say evidence of success?" The president responded, "What are your measurable goals? What growth or improvements can you demonstrate? How are the customers benefiting? How is the company benefiting?"

The young manager admitted he did not have the answers to the company president's questions. As a result of this interaction, Jack recognized that he had some work to do in studying the value-added impact of his project team for the good of the company.

Jack's story is far too prevalent in business, industry, medical and nonprofit organizations today. We are fairly good at implementing change, but we are not as effective at measuring the results of the change. Had Jack been doing a good job of assessing his project team's performance, he could have responded to the president another way. "Sales are up 22%, productivity is up 125%, absenteeism has dropped to 1%, and lost sales dropped to less than 5% during the past quarter. This was a record-setting quarter, sir!"

> *To be effective, change must be measurable.*

With that kind of response, the president of the company would have acknowledged the success in Jack's *success* story.

What is your plan to assess the results of your change initiative? How will you know you have accomplished the strategic goals?

Objective v. Subjective

Effective assessment flows out of specific, measurable goals. This means that to be fair and meaningful, assessment should be based on measurable performance results rather than subjective criteria. Consider the following examples that contrast objective (workable) goals and subjective (unrealistic) goals:

Subjective Goal: Improve support of the sales effort.

Objective Goal: Reduce the time lapse between order date and delivery by 10 percent (two days).

Subjective Goal: Improve the training effort of the office sales staff.

Objective Goal: Provide sales training to 100 percent of the office staff, resulting in an average increase in sales of 5 percent within the first full quarter after the training.

The subjective goals above are too vague and too difficult to measure. The objective goals are specific and measurable. Well-written, clear and measurable goals help to establish clear performance expectations.

The chances of success are greatly enhanced when we enable those directly involved to help set the goals and assess the results. As Sam Walton puts it, "High expectations are the key to everything."[10] Leaders "expect results" while managers "inspect operations."

People should be challenged, but not unduly stressed; stretched, but not broken. When people are challenged to develop shared goals, they will give their best efforts to achieve excellent results. Their high expectations will culminate in exuberant celebration.

As you embark upon this journey to make a significant difference, keep in mind the many kinds of people in this world. There are those . . .

- who think or say I won't.
- who think or say I can't.
- who think or say I will.
- who think or say I am.
- who think or say **I did.**

The goal is to find the doers—mission-motivated people who will join you in saying, **"We're glad we did."**

Endnotes

1. Tom Logsdon, *Breaking Through* (New York: Addison-Wesley Publishing Company, 1993), 8.
2. Adapted from *Celebrating Excellence*, 98.
3. Ibid., 48.
4. *Breaking Through*, 179.
5. Zig Ziglar, *See You at the Top* (Gretna, LA: Pelican Publishing, 1982), 14.
6. *The Fifth Discipline Fieldbook*, 3.
7. *Breaking Through*, 71.
8. James O. Nichols, *A Practitioner's Handbook for Institutional Effectiveness and Student Outcomes Assessment Implementation*, 3rd ed. (Edison, NJ: Agathon Press, 1996), 7-8.
9. Required of all institutions accredited by the North Central Association of Colleges and Schools.
10. *Breaking Through*, 157.

Learning Activities—Chapter 7

What gets thoughtfully and strategically implemented, monitored, and measured gets done with greater results.

1. There is a huge difference between saying "I can" and "we're glad we did." "I can" is an attitude. "I will" is intent. "I am" is taking action toward an assignment or goal. And, "we are glad we did" is the result of team playing in achieving a major goal or creating major change that causes more good things to happen in the organization. Think of a time when you were part of a team and you accomplished the goal or created the constructive change you set out to make happen.
   a. Share your story with some friends or co-workers.
   b. What causal factors made this a success story?
   c. What positive emotions are attached to this success story?
2. Study the questions on page 161. Take a few minutes to thoughtfully answer the six questions. Record your responses in the Leading Change Journal.
3. In what ways has this helped to strengthen your strategic plan for Being the Best for the World, Inc.?

∾ Notes & Ideas ∾

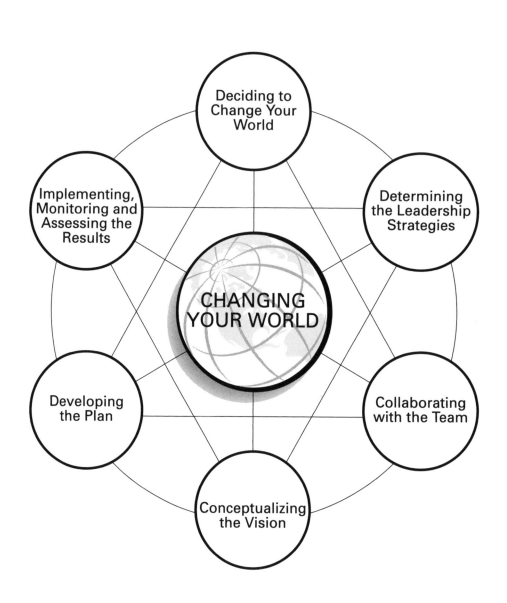

8

STAYING
THE COURSE
Overcoming Obstacles

> *"For every obstacle there is a way—*
> *over, under, around, or through.*
> *So when you have begun a good project,*
> *'Never, Never, Never Quit.'"* [1]
>
> ✎ *attributed to Winston Churchill*

An Indomitable Spirit

Life is not easy. Neither is change and its corresponding challenges. In the process of creating a better world there may be trials, tests and even tribulations. There almost certainly will be resistance, hindrances and obstacles. Even go-getters can be beaten down by such difficulties. But servant leaders aren't just go-getters. They are "go-givers" who use their passion, purpose and inspiration to overcome barriers on the pathway of successful change. They abide by Churchill's famous words: "Never give in—never, never,

"Never give in—never, never, never, never, in nothing great or small."
– W. Churchill

never, never, in nothing great or small, large or petty, never give in except to convictions of honour and good sense."[2]

Although go-givers realize the pathway is narrow, winding and blocked by obstacles, they have a fighting determination—a resolve to stay the course and get the job done. Go-givers demonstrate an indomitable spirit over fear, threat, distraction and perplexing challenges.

MAKING IT PERSONAL:
Lesson in Perseverance

Co-author Mark Smith can testify firsthand about the impact obstacles can have on the goals you have set in your life. His dramatic story is best told in his own words:

"The first Sunday in March started as one of the greatest days of my life. I carried my one-year-old son to the car, placed him in the car seat and climbed into our new Taurus with my wife. As we journeyed through Indiana's flat countryside on our way to the church where I was scheduled to speak that morning, our conversation reflected hope and gratitude for the blessings of life we had received. After all, I was 30 years old and happily married. We had been blessed with our first son, I was enjoying my first job in higher education, we were planning to buy our first home, and I was only months from finishing my dissertation. We were happy and enjoying life just as it should be. After a forty-five-minute, exhilarating drive, we arrived at the church. Part of my message focused on God's sufficient grace for us in times of discouragement. I told the congregation that even in our most difficult situations, God will be the sustaining force in our lives. Little did I realize what lay ahead and how true that exhortation was going to be for me personally.

"After we shared lunch with a kind church family, I left my wife and son and headed to a board meeting. I got into my car and had traveled only about four miles when I was hit head-on by another car. My vehicle spun a number of times and then skidded one hundred twenty feet. I don't know how long I was unconscious, perhaps only a few moments, but when I did regain some consciousness I remember asking someone to please phone my wife. Trapped in the car with smoke billowing all around me, I was suddenly overwhelmed by the thought that I was going to die. In fact, I remember calling out, 'Oh God, I am dying!' This was immediately followed by the comforting presence of the Holy Spirit and I knew that while I didn't *want* to die, I was *ready* to die.

"But I didn't die. I was pulled from the wreckage and taken to a hospital, where the doctors found that I couldn't walk. This accident put many obstacles in my path. Here I was— beginning a new career in higher education, about to defend my dissertation in three weeks—and I could not even move my left side from the waist down. Suddenly, everything seemed to be on hold as I battled for my life.

"But with God's grace, I did not give up. The road back to recovery was a long, painful journey. It involved many surgeries and three hours of physical therapy every day for a year. I learned to walk again, battling obstacles one at a time and progressing (literally and figuratively) step by step.

"I defended and completed my dissertation from my bed. I continued my academic career and have been promoted on four occasions. With hard work and God's grace, I overcame the obstacles in my pathway and changed my world."

Perseverance is an essential quality for world changers. Much good that might have been achieved in the world is lost through procrastination, hesitation, vacillation or simply not persevering in the face of obstacles and resistance. Mark's story is a wonderful example of perseverance. He not only overcame every obstacle in his path to a full and productive life and the subsequent challenges of recovery, but he prevailed. He willfully and indefatigably demonstrated the spirit of determination in prevailing over significant, life-altering challenges—challenges that could have defeated a go-getter but which brought out the best in this go-giver!

Perseverance is an essential quality for world changers.

Force-Field Analysis

According to Kurt Lewin's "force field" theory,[3] every behavior is the result of a dynamic tension between driving (facilitating) forces and restraining forces. The facilitating forces push toward the intended results. The restraining forces push toward failure. The challenge is to increase the facilitating forces while decreasing the restraining forces in order to achieve the intended results.

Force-field analysis is a somewhat simple tool in dealing with the complexity and uncertainty of change. However, it can be a very useful tool in identifying the obstacles to change in moving from current reality to the intended result.

Narrowing the Focus

A force-field analysis begins with two focusing questions:

1. What are the resistances, obstacles and restraining forces that can deter us from accomplishing our strategic plan? That is, how can we prevent failure?
2. What resources must be brought to bear on facilitating productive change? That is, what will enable the intended results? (See figure 8.1.)

FIGURE 8.1

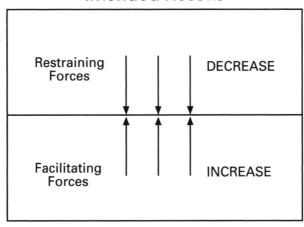

Intended Results

173

Adapting Force-field Analysis to your Change Process

Your change facilitation team can adapt Lewin's force-field analysis to its strategic plan. To implement this useful resource, take the following steps:

1. Brainstorm a list of all the restraining forces your team can anticipate as it implements the strategic plan.
2. Carefully evaluate this list and prioritize the restraining forces that should be dealt with at this stage of implementation.
3. List all of the facilitating (i.e., enabling or driving) forces.
4. Carefully evaluate this list and prioritize the facilitating forces that should be dealt with at this stage of implementation.
5. Establish actions for decreasing the prioritized restraining actions and for increasing the facilitative actions.
6. Divide the labor and begin harnessing the positive forces that enable productive change.

As your change facilitation team communicates the vision, executes the strategic plan and monitors the change process, it needs to anticipate obstacles and resistance. Much resistance comes about because of the very nature of the change process. As we have outlined earlier, the whole idea of change can intimidate many people. How your change facilitation team manages this concept is key to its success in fulfilling its strategic plan.

The Challenge of Change

In Chapter 1, we look at how people view change. Some see change as an opportunity for growth. Others resist change and view it negatively. Change is so challenging because people must carry on with their lives and their work while managing the processes of change that directly affect their day-to-day responsibilities. Added to this, the complexity of our fast-paced culture makes it difficult to anticipate every obstacle, resistance or hindrance to productive change. Among the things that can stymie the change process are these realities:

- Many people are fearful of change.
- Change challenges the status quo.
- Many individuals will resist change.
- Coping with uncertainty and risk is stressful.
- Many people are not sold on the need for change.
- Trust is lacking between the leaders and the led.
- Lifestyle, culture, systems and routine procedures can be obstacles to change.
- Boards, leaders, agencies, policies and regulations can hinder change.
- New knowledge, skills, principles and practices may need to be developed.
- The change facilitation team can become weary in well-doing and give up.

Change is not easy, but productive change can make our world a better place. Among change's biggest opponents are complacency, obsolescence and inertia. As you embark upon a strategic plan to change an issue in your world, remember Ross Perot's admonition: "Most people give up just when they're about to achieve success. They quit on the one-yard line. They give up at the last minute of the game, one foot from a winning touchdown."[4]

The Four Stages of Change

Why is it so difficult for some people to change or so easy for others to quit during the process of change? Change experts Cynthia D. Scott and Dennis T. Jaffe[5] have studied change in organizations and groups through the years. They note that during significant change everyone goes through four stages:

1. Denial
2. Resistance
3. Exploration
4. Commitment

Generally people experience these four stages in the same order. Whether influencing individuals, groups or organizations, the agent of change will need to understand that different people will experience these four stages in different degrees and with varied outcomes. Some people quickly find their way to *commitment,* whereas others may get stymied at the *resistance* stage. Sensitivity to the needs of individuals is very important during the change process.

Michael Blumenthal, former CEO of Unisys, says, "Some people really get scared when change occurs. Maybe they shouldn't but they do. You have to be able to relate to that and say to yourself, 'I have to be tolerant of that and I have to assuage it, and channel it constructively.'"[6]

Coping with Denial

Some people enjoy change. Others do not. However, nearly everyone, including people who enjoy change, will confront the denial stage. Change for the individual or the group can be threatening. It may suggest that we are not doing something well or correctly. It will probably require some new attitudes, knowledge and skills. It may mean a different mindset or compel us to establish new relationships. The key is that an agent of change must be sensitive in order to help people cope with whatever change they are experiencing. To help people or groups through the denial phase, the change agent must:

- **Listen**—really listen to the spirit/voice/content of what people are saying. Be sensitive to their needs.
- **Collaborate**—establish a trusting relationship, a sense of collaboration.
- **Communicate**—communicate the vision, benefits and desired results frequently and consistently.
- **Mentor**—teach, mentor and coach people continuously.

Avoiding the Abyss of Resistance

Some people view change as being in an abyss out of which they may never climb. The forces keeping them down include resistance, fear, defensiveness and procrastination. Not even the "rule of holes" can assuage these change resisters: when you find yourself in a hole, quit digging.

For others the abyss is more like a foxhole or cocoon. They feel very safe and comfortable where they are. They have trouble seeing that life outside the abyss can be better because of productive change.

177

The change agent can help people successfully work through the resistance stage by

- getting them to see that the vision is **attainable** (it must be clear and convincing and it must be theirs);
- transmitting **honesty** and integrity so that the change agent and the vision are seen to be trustworthy;
- recognizing that it takes inner strength and **courage** to work through personal or professional change;
- **cooperating**, collaborating and celebrating every step on the road to successful change.

The Excitement of Exploration

By the time people have worked through the denial and resistance stages of change, they have overcome inertia and are gaining momentum. As they climb out of the abyss, a mountain may confront them—but they sense that they can climb it, assured that things will only get better. They have achieved a breakthrough and are ready to press forward toward the desired vision. Maneuvering successfully through the exploration stage requires certain guidelines:

- Don't move too quickly. It takes **time** to change attitudes, know-how and skills. It takes time to form new habits.
- Recognize and celebrate short-term gains. Acknowledge and **share success** vignettes openly.
- Encourage ongoing reflection and **feedback.** Be sensitive when making course corrections or when confronted with roadblocks (obstacles).

- Build on successes. Keep **hope** alive.

Making the Commitment

The fourth stage of change is commitment to continuous improvement. Without commitment the change cannot be institutionalized. Commitment is both a decision and a process. The leader of the change facilitation team must enable a spirit of collaboration, a commitment to continuous improvement, and a team

> *The fourth stage of change is commitment to continuous improvement.*

culture aimed at producing excellent results. There must be a prevailing attitude that this is a worthwhile change initiative that will produce enduring results and benefits for all stakeholders. The attitude is one that communicates to those being empowered by the change initiative that "anything worth doing is worth doing imperfectly until we can do it perfectly." In other words, there is an eagerness to bring about the desired results and a willingness to do it now, even when it becomes necessary to make some course corrections based on feedback during the process of implementing the change strategy.

The leader of the change facilitation team recognizes the following criteria for obtaining commitment to continuous improvement:

- The change initiative will require commitment from the top or approval to proceed with the process.
- The change facilitation team must fully understand and buy in to the change. They must trust the leader and share in the vision of the change project.
- The change facilitation team leader and members will need

to ask themselves, "Are we wholly committed to this change project?"

- The change facilitation members must value teamwork and have a clear vision and well-thought-through strategic and operational plan to produce the intended results.

- The change facilitation team must have a "Can Do" spirit. They must believe in the vision and clearly see the attainment of the goals. Once internalized, this spirit, vision and creative energy will produce astounding results.

Is It a Problem or a PROBLEM?

Part of dealing with change has to do with how you view it. Is it a threat or a challenge? Is it a problem or an opportunity?

Leadership author and motivational teacher John Maxwell has a unique way of looking at obstacles, resistance and hindrances to change.[7] He uses an acrostic to highlight the significance of **PROBLEMS**. This acrostic adapts very nicely to our world-changing concepts:

- **Predictor.** The perceived problem becomes a predictor of the magnitude of the potential solution's impact. The greater the size and challenge of the problem, the greater the predictability that the solution will make a huge impact upon people and organizations.

- **Reminders.** Problems remind us of our reason for being world changers. Problems challenge us to pull together in making our world a better place to live. They remind us of our need to be connected with the greatest Problem Solver of all time.

- **Opportunities.** Problems are simply opportunities for us to activate our talents for the benefit of people and organizations. In Chinese the symbols for crisis and opportunity are the same. In effect, crisis becomes an opportunity for those committed to making a difference in the world.

Predictor

Reminders

Opportunities

Blessings

Lessons

Everywhere

Messages

Solvable

– John Maxwell

- **Blessings.** Problems in the world remind us to count our blessings daily. One of the keys to being a world changer is to be thankful for the many blessings in our lives. This in turn stirs our hearts to be a blessing to others—to use our talents, abilities and resources to make a difference in our world.

- **Lessons.** Problems teach us the lessons of patience, interdependency, perseverance and persistence. As we resolve problems in our lives, we learn lessons that on another day at another time will enable us to help people solve their problems. Experience is one of life's greatest teachers.

- **Everywhere.** Problems are everywhere. And so are solutions. A loser sees the glass as half empty. A winner sees the glass as half full. A world changer sees that there are thirsty, needy, hurting people everywhere—people who simply need to drink the water from that glass. Our challenge is to reach out and meet that need.

- **Messages.** Problems are messages that remind us of our mission and calling in life. In sensitively meeting the needs of others, we respond to their SOS message. By committing to create a better way and place for them, we send a message back by our example and our shared success stories, proving that we can make this world a better place.

• **Solvable.** There is a solution to every problem. Our challenge is a quest for solutions that enable ordinary people to do extraordinary things on behalf of mankind.

We applaud the problem solvers who take risks and overcome obstacles in order to make a better world for all of us. Coping with major problems and obstacles, relying on God's help and working in harmony with others, they turn a problem into a solution, a crisis into an opportunity, a need into a fulfillment.

What Is a Prevailer?

The world is made up of three types of people: survivors, overcomers, and prevailers. Lance Armstrong understands the difference between these categories. A world-class cyclist, he was unexpectedly stricken with cancer in his prime. Refusing to be defeated by this life-threatening disease, he fought with courage and tenacity for his very survival. With the aid of modern medicine and his fighting determination, he returned to competitive cycling and won the 1999 Tour de France. This grueling twenty-three-day race covers 2,125 miles of challenging, mountainous terrain. In 2000 he returned and won again, as he did in 2001, 2002, 2003, 2004 and 2005, becoming the only cyclist in the world to win seven consecutive Tours, "confirming him as the greatest cyclist ever."[8]

What distinguishes a prevailer from a survivor or overcomer?

- **Faith**—Prevailers have faith in God. They live their lives according to a strong belief system. They realize that those who say "I can" and those who say "I can't" are both right. They not only believe that the best is yet to come, they know deep down that the best has already begun.

- **Understanding**—Prevailers understand who they are, why they exist and what they want to accomplish in life. Moreover, they seek to really understand others and are sensitive to their needs. They have an uncommon sense of knowing when and how to do kind and courageous acts of service for others.

- **Perseverance**—Prevailers understand and practice the "law of perseverance." They have an inner resolve to stay the course. They refuse to quit or be stopped by obstacles. They believe the simple adage that when the going gets tough, the tough get going.

- **Flexibility**—Prevailers are both creative and flexible. They are principled individuals. However, they understand the need for responsiveness and know-how to harness the creative, optimistic energy to flexibly overcome obstacles and resistance in the process.

- **Resilience**—Prevailers are resilient people. They have personally survived to thrive. They know that determination and domination over the obstacles set before them can result in victory over the challenge.

- **Momentum**—Prevailers are sensitive to the strongholds of complacency and inertia in people and organizations. They earnestly seek ways to establish momentum (i.e., positive movement toward the desired goal) and celebrate short-term gains. They share those stories to build greater momentum in bringing about creative change.

This brief overview of the six qualities of prevailers clearly shows the importance of one's character and mental attitude in bringing about constructive change and inventive solutions to problems. Prevailers respond rather than react to the challenges of helping people and organizations improve. They understand this promise of Jesus from John 16:33 ANT:

> *In the world you have tribulation and trials and distress and frustration; but be of good cheer [take courage; be confident, certain, undaunted]! For I have overcome the world. [I have deprived it of power to harm you and have conquered it for you].*

The English word "overcome" in the Greek language is "nike," which means to conquer, prevail and succeed. The key to moving from survival to success is the willingness to change and be a leader of change.

The Sources of Resistance

Obstacles or resistance to change within an organization can come from internal or external sources. The challenge to the world changer is to be able to work with and through the obstacles and resistance.

Individual Sources

Moorhead and Griffin note six individual sources of change and offer examples of each:[9]

Individual Sources	Examples
Habit	Changing tasks, settings, and processes
Security	Altering the culture, systems, and work routines

184

Economic Factors	Changes in pay, benefits, and payment schedules
Fear of the Unknown	New job responsibilities, change of department, new supervisor, new technology, new company owner
Lack of Awareness	Poor communication of change, people working in isolation, isolated work units, poor education and training
Social Factors	Employee turnover, changing group norms, tacky supervisors

Organizational Sources

In addition to individual sources of change, there are organizational sources of resistance to change.[10] While these may vary from organization to organization, they reflect things an agent of change should be looking for when implementing constructive change.

Organizational Sources	**Examples**
Overdetermination	Employment system, job descriptions, evaluation and reward system
Narrow Focus of Change	Structure changed with no concern given to other issues; e.g., jobs, people
Group Inertia	Group norms
Threatened Expertise	People move out of area of expertise
Threatened Power	Decentralized decision making
Resource Allocation	Increased use of part-time help

Barriers to Change

We can group the barriers to change into three general categories:[11]

1. Barriers to understanding—not fully understanding what is proposed
2. Barriers to acceptance—those affected will not accept the change
3. Barriers to acting—factors inhibiting implementation

An agent of change will be quick to discover creative ways to promote understanding, acceptance and clear-cut actions in order to effectively implement change within a group or organization. Sensitivity, communication, monitoring, feedback and course correction are facilitating factors in dealing with the barriers to understanding, acceptance and acting.

Rest in Your Believing

Once you have strategically charted your course for the world-changing project you have envisioned, it is of the utmost importance to exercise patience and diligence in the implementation, monitoring and assessment stage. Be sure not to be *restless in your achieving* but to *rest in your believing*. Restlessness, anxiety, worry and doubt all can become obstacles in the passionate pursuit of change. Restlessness will result in other obstacles being thrown in the pathway of your pursuit. Restlessness

Patience becomes of paramount importance for the agent of change.

- magnifies the obstacles and resistance;
- creates tension and negative energy for you and others;
- causes "paralysis of analysis";
- distracts you from your primary decisions;
- costs you what patience can save you (haste makes waste);
- takes you where you don't want to go.

Patience becomes of paramount importance for the agent of change. Through nature's example, God eloquently teaches us the law of the harvest. You plant the seed—begin the implementation plan, recognize that worthwhile projects take time—and then patiently await the harvest, the successful culmination of the project. The law of the harvest is a simple equation:

Seed + Time = Harvest

The miracle of Mark's long road to recovery and restoration was his optimism, patience and diligence. He made the decision to recover, believed he could overcome this tragedy, and cooperated with doctors and therapists. He planted the seed for full recovery and God produced the miracle. He *rested in his believing* and he never, never, never lost faith or gave up. As a result, he overcame this setback and is prevailing in the game of life once again.

Endnotes

1. Attributed to Winston Churchill, as quoted in *Celebrating Excellence,* 100.

2. October 29, 1941, Winston Churchill, in a speech to the boys of Harrow School, the school he once attended as a boy. Retrieved October 17, 2000, from "Famous Quotes & Stories of Winston Churchill," © The Churchill Center Inc. Home Page on the World Wide Web at http://www.winstonchurchill.org.

3. Kurt Lewin, *Field Theory in Social Science,* ed. D. Cartwright (New York: Harper and Row Brokers, 1951).

4. *Celebrating Excellence,* 71.

5. *The Healthy Company,* 106.

6. Ibid.

7. From a 1996 speech at Indiana Wesleyan University, Marion, IN.

8. "Armstrong's last ride ends with victory," ESPN Olympic Sports online, *Tour de France* (July 25, 2005). Found at http://sports.espn.go.com/oly/tdf2005/news/story?id=2115344 (retrieved February 12, 2007).

9. *Organizational Behavior,* 556.

10. Katz and Kahn as quoted in Moorhead and Griffin, *Organizational Behavior,* 556.

11. Patrick E. Connor and Linda K. Lake, *Managing Organizational Change* (New York: Praeger Publishers, 1982), 187.

Learning Activities—Chapter 8

If it is to be it is up to the HE in me.

1. Think of a time you gave up on a goal or quit working on a major project that you now wish you had completed. Think of how many times you may have said, "Why didn't I . . . ?" Or, "I wish I would have . . ."
   a. Why did you give up?
   b. How do you still feel about that issue?

2. Winston Churchill said, "Never give in—never, never, never, never, in nothing great or small, large or petty, never give in except to convictions of honour and good sense" (Churchill speech, 1941, see p. 170) Now, think of a time when you accomplished a major goal and completed a challenging assignment quite well.
   a. What inspired you to keep on keeping on—to persevere?
   b. Who collaborated with you or encouraged you along the way?
   c. How did that make you feel? Record these in your Leading Change Journal.

3. Refer to the Assessment Model—Figure 7.1 (p. 159). In order to assess the intended results, answer the following six focusing questions. Record these in your Leading Change Journal.
   a. How does your SMART *goal* now read? (Be sure it is specific and results focused.)
   b. What *measures* might I use to determine the successful accomplishment of this goal?
   c. What *performance indicators* will serve as acceptable evidence I have successfully accomplished the goal? (That is to say, how will I know I have accomplished the goal?)
   d. What *accountability coaching data* do I plan to gather along the way to successfully accomplish the goal?
   e. What was the compelling need or problem I was trying to resolve? How does the new data or evidence of progress *compare with the data* that undergirded the initial need or problem?
   f. What course corrections or *recommended changes* do I need to make to ensure successful accomplishment of the goal?

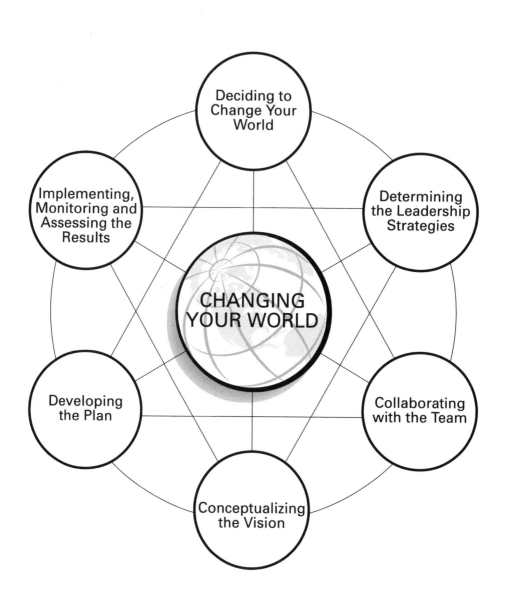

Deciding to Change Your World

Determining the Leadership Strategies

Collaborating with the Team

Conceptualizing the Vision

Developing the Plan

Implementing, Monitoring and Assessing the Results

CHANGING YOUR WORLD

9

GET UP AND
GET GOING
Building a Brighter Tomorrow

*"I shall pass through this world but once. If,
therefore, there be any kindness I can show, or any
good thing I can do, let me do it now; let me not defer
it or neglect it, for I shall not pass this way again."*[1]

∽ *Attributed to Etienne de Grellet*

Profound Questions

What would make your life more
worthwhile? How might you help
others find more meaningful,
productive and fulfilling lives? How
might you do your fair share in making
this world a better place to live? What is the noblest thing you could
do to make a real difference in your circle of influence?

These are profound questions of the heart and mind. They stem

*Can you imagine having
a "bright tomorrow"
so you can lead others
to one, too?*

not just from a need to find meaning in life, but from a need to align your life with purpose.

Together these questions ask how you are responding to your life's purpose.

MAKING IT PERSONAL:
Merging Job with Life Mission

Linda was a single parent of two grown children. She had worked at a manufacturing plant for twenty-two years and was within eight years of retirement at the time she enrolled in a motivation, development, and change course. During the first session of the course, the instructor asked how many of the students had written a mission statement. He asked, "In what way does your life mission merge with your job?" The instructor then directed the students to spend some quality time over the next few days jotting down a few phrases that would reflect what they perceived their professional mission statements to be—why they do what they do.

In what way does your life mission merge with your job?

At first Linda thought this was not only a ridiculous task but an invasion of privacy as well. And yet, deep inside she knew that she was not happy with her work. In fact, she had grown cynical about her workplace and had difficulty trusting her manager and some of his inner circle. So Linda took one evening to really think about her professional mission. Her jot list included some of the following phrases:

• To be treated equally with men in the workplace

- To be paid equally with men in the workplace
- To be promoted two levels higher than my current position before retirement
- To build my retirement fund to a level that would enable me to maintain a high standard of living
- To prove to management that I deserve promotion

As Linda studied her list she began to see how miserable she was. She was frustrated with her boss and obsessed with climbing the company ladder. She realized how vain her subconscious mission was and she recognized that she was part of the problem. As a result, Linda really began to think about what her life purpose should be. In the process she recognized how lonely and unappreciative she had become over the years, due to her drive to earn lots of money and prove herself in the workplace. She asked herself, "What do I really want to accomplish during my lifetime?" And then she decided it was time to "get up and get going."

After brainstorming a number of thoughts and writing three or four mission statements, Linda came up with this: *"My mission in life is to have an intimate relationship with the Lord, to have a sense of purpose from my job, and to do acts of kindness for others."* She then listed four core values that she wanted reflected in all she did. Her core values were *trust, peace of mind, kindness, and total well-being.*

Excited about her mission and core values, Linda immediately began writing goals and action steps to enable her to actualize her life mission and core values in all she did. The following week Linda could hardly wait to tell her story

What do I really want to accomplish during my lifetime?

of transformation. She asked the instructor if she could share her mission, core values and goals with the class. When she finished speaking, she was given a standing ovation.

Linda's story does not end there. Using the PISCO model she developed a strategic plan to begin changing the work culture within her sphere of influence at the manufacturing plant. Her manager and the plant manager approved a Project Team with Linda as the team leader to assess the department culture where Linda had worked for the past nine years.

Linda got up and got going—changing her life and making a dramatic change in her world.

It's Not Just a Dream

We have recently entered a new millennium. We can do more than just *wonder* and *dream* about what the world will be like in five years or ten years, or what it might be like for our children and grandchildren. We can do two positive things:

1. We can pray for and believe in a better, happier, healthier, safer world.
2. We can decide to make a better, happier, healthier, safer world.

Our decision to make the world a better place for everyone begins internally and ripples outward through our circles of influence—our families, our churches, our communities, our organizations, and ultimately our world.

In this chapter we will reiterate the principal truths we have already studied and balance them against a plan for personal development and accountability. In so doing we hope you will embark on your own exodus, accepting the challenge and implementing the vision to be a world changer.

MAKING IT PERSONAL:
The World Is My Parish!

Near the end of the eighteenth century, England was in decline. Poverty, alcoholism, crime and moral decay ran rampant through the country. Moved by the Holy Spirit a group of students at Oxford University took a stand for holiness. Among those students were Charles and John Wesley. These young men embarked on a deep and thorough study of the Bible's truths until their hearts were on fire for spiritual revival in England.

Our decision to make the world a better place for everyone begins internally.

When they attempted to bring about change in the Church of England, the Church resisted the changes and forbade Wesley to preach in the churches. Undaunted, Wesley turned from the Church and declared, "The world is my parish." He got up and got going with a zealous desire to change the hearts and minds of his countrymen. In the process the Methodist Church was founded.

Revival then spread throughout England and crossed the Atlantic to America. Thousands of people attended great open-air meetings to hear John Wesley share the life-changing challenge to repent and become a believer in Jesus. Before Wesley, England had been on the brink of financial and moral ruin. But when this once mighty kingdom responded at last, England not only experienced spiritual revival but moral and economic revival as well.[2]

This true story demonstrates that we cannot fully know the impact we might have on the lives of people with whom we regularly come into contact, nor can we ever completely comprehend how big or far-reaching our circle of influence will be. Someone who reads this book might become extraordinarily influential as a world changer. At the very least, we hope scores of people who read this book will become agents of positive and constructive change. As we have emphasized throughout the book, it is important to remember that people change before organizations do.

If It Is to Be

Many of us have heard the saying, "If not you, then who? If not now, then when? If not here, then where?" Change begins first with a decision, then a plan, then coordinated action to achieve the goals and vision of the desired change.

Change begins first with a decision, then a plan, then coordinated action to achieve the goals and vision of the desired change.

We may never be as influential as Wesley, Mother Teresa, Gandhi, Martin Luther King, Cesar Chavez, Ronald Reagan or Colin Powell. But each of us can increase our present influence as we respond to the call to become a world changer.

Another popular saying tells us, "If it is to be, it is up to me." We believe this saying is only partially true. We have only to cite Wesley as proof. His heart was set ablaze to become an agent of change, bringing spiritual revival first to the hearts of his countrymen and then to the people of the world. In Wesley's case the saying would read:

"If it is to be, it is up to He in me."

Before the Wesley brothers "got up and got going," they had to have a change of heart. In much the same way Paul personally challenges us with this inspiring promise in 2 Corinthians 5:17-21 CEV:

Anyone who belongs to Christ is a new person. The past is forgotten, and everything is new. God has done it all! He sent Christ to make peace between himself and us, and he has given us the work of making peace between himself and others.

What we mean is that God was in Christ, offering peace and forgiveness to the people of this world. And he has given us the work of sharing his message about peace. We were sent to speak for Christ, and God is begging you to listen to our message. We speak for Christ and sincerely ask you to make peace with God. Christ never sinned! But God treated him as a sinner, so that Christ could make us acceptable to God.

This, then, is our personal challenge:

- Be spiritually mature and morally fit.
- Relate well with as many people as possible.
- Be the best we can be for the world.
- Be rich in kind deeds.
- Be a champion for reconciliation.

197

Putting Principles into Practice

Being a world changer is a daily challenge. It is not so much a goal as it is a day-by-day, step-by-step process. It is not something *outside* or *apart from* us, but something in which we are intimately involved.

> *Becoming a world changer is a daily challenge.*

Two models or "formulas" are worth considering as we look at ways to help us adequately prepare for this daily challenge.

Up, In, and On!

Zig Ziglar made the phrase "Up and On" popular several years ago. He would tell his audiences that while he was always "up" when conducting interviews or speaking before radio and television audiences, he was not always "on." By that he meant that despite his best efforts to prepare his heart and mind properly and prayerfully before a speaking engagement, he sometimes did not fully connect with the audience or "get into the flow."

Ziglar's curiously honest confession has relevance to world changers. We choose to expand this concept to "Up, In, and On." As we seek to optimize the enormous potential for good that resides within each of us, we can take these principles to heart:

- **UP**—the first affection, attitude and action should be to fill up and overflow with the love of God. Look for ways to bubble up and bubble over in all our relationships. Be a wellspring of love and kindness.
- **IN**—the second affection, attitude and action is to be in the Spirit of love. As we daily prepare our hearts and minds

with the right spiritual attitude, we are better able to stay in the Spirit during the day's tough situations.

- **ON**—the third affection, attitude and action is to be grounded in and standing on the Word of truth. As God grants us insight and understanding into spiritual truths, we are increasingly able to draw on the ancient and enduring wisdom of the ages.

Seven Life-Enhancing Habits

In addition to the "Up, In, On" model, we will benefit from cultivating the following life-sustaining, life-enhancing habits:

1. **Start with an Hour of Solitude:** Throughout the recorded history of mankind, we have learned that the greatest and most influential people have mastered the practice of solitude, contemplative thinking or prayer— a practice that puts them in position to experience the presence of the Lord. This hour of solitude, preferably the first hour of the day, is sometimes affectionately referred to as the "golden hour." The first hour can help you chart your course for the day, set the sail and pick up the wind to carry you cheerfully and productively through the day.

2. **Read Your Mission Statement and Major Goals:** Successful people have mission statements defining who they *passionately* want to be. They also write down major goals that include action steps and desired benefits. These tools enable them to know and do the important things they

199

have charted for their lives. The world is made up of takers and givers, dividers and multipliers, losers and winners, world changers for evil and world changers for good. The givers, multipliers, winners and world changers for constructive good in the lives and organizations of the world have clear and concise mission statements. They regularly set and reach important goals that will benefit mankind.

3. **Plan Your Day and Live Your Plan:** Edward de Bono wrote, "Thinking is the ultimate human resource. Yet we can never be satisfied with our most important skill. No matter how good we become, we should always want to be better."[3] Meditative, contemplative, creative, reflective and strategic thinking are the skills and practices that set the servant leaders and world changers apart from the other 75 percent to 90 percent of the world's population. A daily planning ritual, involving only five to fifteen minutes of time will enable you to identify key areas of focus for that particular day. It will help you to act rather than react. It gives you a framework that allows for flexibility as the day unfolds. Working with a plan is not only personally fulfilling, it allows you the time to accomplish more for others.

4. **Keep the Main Thing the Main Thing:** A popular adage exhorts, "Be here now." That is to say, focus on what you are doing this moment. Joe Durant is quoted as saying, "I was able to stay in the present."[4] There is truth in that. Broken focus ends in failure, while concentrated focus produces success. Steven Covey has popularized a time

management strategy that analyzes how people spend their day. He breaks daily activities into four quadrants:[5]

Figure 9.1	Four Quadrants of Daily Activity
I. Urgent and Important ❏ Unanticipated problems ❏ Mandates ❏ Changed end dates ❏ People conflict ❏ Technology breakdown ❏ Emergencies	II. Not Urgent, but Important ❏ Relating collegially ❏ Vital daily responsibilities ❏ Decision making ❏ Progress on reports ❏ Important calls ❏ Important correspondence
III. Urgent and Not Important ❏ Calls from home, just to talk ❏ Calls from a friend, just to talk ❏ Walk-in interruptions ❏ Time wasters	IV. Not Urgent and Not Important ❏ Small talk with friends ❏ Reading unrelated information ❏ Surfing the Internet ❏ Extended coffee breaks

Source: Based on Stephen Covey, *The 7 Habits of Highly Effective People: Powerful Lessons in Personal Change* (New York: A Fireside Book, 1990), 151.

Your challenge is to plan your day and focus your thoughts on the best use of your time. In the process you can proactively spend more time in the Not Urgent, but Important quadrant. Of course urgent, unanticipated things will sometimes arise. However, the goal is to focus as much as possible on the important things that will produce the greatest benefit for the greatest number of people.

5. **Renew and Expand Your Mind:** The most influential people in the world build this into their schedules—they regularly seek opportunities to renew, refresh and expand their minds. They are avid readers of good books

and journals. When driving they listen to uplifting and informational tapes and CD's. Many view inspirational videotapes while using exercise equipment or listen to audiocassette tapes while cycling, jogging or walking. They seize the opportunity to expand their knowledge and update their skills. They recognize the wisdom in the proverb we quoted earlier: *"Any enterprise is built by wise planning, becomes strong through common sense, and profits wonderfully by keeping abreast of the facts."* (Proverbs 24:3-4 LB).

6. **Practice Reflective Assessment:** Highly influential people frequently ask two questions after significant experiences or encounters with others:

1. "What did I do well?"

2. "What would I do differently next time?"

This practice of reflective assessment enables them to continuously improve their connection to people with whom they work or interact on a regular basis. Better connections facilitate better results. While it is important to achieve goals and positive results on a daily basis, it is vitally important to achieve these goals or produce these positive results in a way that benefits all concerned. There are times when goal achievement serves the goal-setter, but does not produce goodwill or directly benefit the others involved. As we noted in the fourth habit above, the goal is to focus as much as possible on the important things that will produce the greatest benefit for the greatest number of people. Healthy, caring relationships and trust are keys to being the goal achiever and world changer you desire to become.

7. **Treat Every Person as a VIP:** The first step in this habit is to know that we are loved and valued by God and are called to transmit that Spirit of love to others. *If it is to be it is up to He in me.* The second step is to treat every person as a Very Important Person (VIP). This is the principle of the "Golden Rule" and the "Royal Law of Love."

The Four-Way Test

Herbert Taylor, an extraordinarily influential Christian businessman, developed what is known as "The Four-Way Test." Taylor was energetic, success-oriented, inventive, hardworking, honest, sensitive, loving and a deeply religious leader. Popularized by Rotary International, Taylor's Four-Way Test is suggested as a filter through which we should pass everything we say, do or plan. Simple, direct and remarkably profound, Taylor's words should resonate in our hearts:

This simple test is the key to treating every person as a VIP.

1. Is it the truth?
2. Is it fair to all concerned?
3. Will it build goodwill and better friendships?
4. Will it be beneficial to all concerned?[6]

This simple test is the key to treating every person as a VIP. The four-way test can be applied to your family relationships, in the workplace and in your church or community.

It's Time for Action!

No matter how small we may perceive our circle of influence to be, we need to rise above complacency and inaction to make a difference in the lives and organizations of our world. What might be daunting to an individual can be achieved through a unified effort. Working together we have the collective intelligence, vision and power (influence) to turn back the tide of moral decay, apathy and aimlessness that is so prevalent in our world.

Critical Issues

If we need to be reminded of the critical issues and desperate needs of our world, we need look no farther than these—many of which can be found in our own communities:

- Dysfunctional families
- Millions of "at-risk" children and adults
- Illiteracy
- Rundown and unsafe neighborhoods
- Homeless men, women and youth
- Racial tension
- Cultural warfare
- All manner of addictions
- Abortion
- Crime
- Educational underachievement
- Poor morale in the workplace

The issues are plentiful and the problems are great, but so are the opportunities. Take a moment and reflect upon some of your earlier goals and plans. Have you begun implementing, monitoring and measuring those plans? Are there new and more important change projects for which you might be the initiator? Is there a compelling issue from the list above that seems to be calling to you? If so, circle the issue or issues for which you might have a suggestion or solution. As you review the list, are there other compelling issues or inspired ideas that seem to be tugging at you? If so, make note of them.

Inspiring Examples

No problem is too big to tackle, no issue too impossible to resolve. We can reach across the social, cultural, racial, economic and religious gaps that tend to divide us and restore a sense of community. We can do our fair share and renew our commitment of service to people and organizations. Others have done it, some of them working with fewer resources than we have available.

- **Isis T. Johnson.** When she was only four years old, she approached her grandmother and asked if they could send their chickens to the starving children in Ethiopia. Today, the Isis T. Johnson Foundation organizes food and clothing drives for the needy in many communities.[7]
- **Joanne Alter.** She became concerned about the problems in Chicago's public schools and volunteered to help in a classroom. She then began a program called "Working in the Schools" (WITS), which finds volunteers or corporate partners to help children read.[8]
- **Secretary of State Colin Powell.** He identified as many as

fifteen million "at-risk" American youth. As chairman of America's Promise—The Alliance for Youth, he worked to disseminate information about and seek resolution to this crisis. America's Promise is an alliance of hundreds of organizations that have committed to the goal of ensuring that at least two million additional young people between the ages of infancy to twenty years of age are connected to five fundamental resources: a healthy start, safe places to live, adult mentors, training in marketable skills, and opportunities to serve.[9]

There are hundreds of stories like these and thousands of kind and courageous people willing to help meet the critical needs of America. You can make a difference by joining with an existing organization or creating a world-changing project of your own. It is quite possible that your project could grow into an organization. Consider these questions:

1. If you could make a difference in someone's life, what would you do?
2. If you could make a difference among the aging, what would you do?
3. If you could make a difference in your neighborhood, community, school district or church, what would you do?
4. If you could make a difference in helping "at-risk" youth or adults, what would you do?
5. If you could make a difference in your workplace, what would you do?
6. If you could make a difference in local, state or national government, what would you do?

The Law of Reciprocity

The soundtrack of the film *Sleepless in Seattle* includes these lyrics from an old Jimmy Durante song: "Make someone happy. Make just one someone happy and you will be happy too!"

Choose to exchange the ordinary for the extraordinary.

That song captures perfectly the "law of reciprocity." As we give of ourselves to others, we receive just as much or more in return.

Earlier, you set some personal/professional goals. You were also encouraged to identify a problem or an opportunity worthy of a strategic plan. Now is the time to embark seriously upon that plan.

R. Buckminster Fuller wrote, "Each human has his lifetime to invest—to realize the potentials of her various freedoms and choices, to be employed to the advantage of all human beings, in order that we may fulfill our mission on this planet."[10]

Get Up and Go-Give

"Each time a man stands up for an ideal, or acts to improve the life of others, or strikes out against injustice," Robert F. Kennedy said, "he sends a tiny ripple of hope, and those ripples, crossing each other from a million different centers of energy, build a current which can sweep down the mightiest walls of oppression and resistance."[11]

It is your time to stand for an ideal and to act courageously to improve the

"Each time a man stands up for an ideal, or acts to improve the life of others, or strikes out against injustice, he sends a tiny ripple of hope."
— Robert F. Kennedy

207

lives of others. Our most heartfelt desire is that through this book you have been drawn into an integrated experience of intellectual challenge, leadership development, spiritual growth and renewal in becoming a world changer. As you begin your journey, we challenge you to make the time to listen, really listen for your "call."

Each of the world's problems has a solution. Each of the world's opportunities can be fully realized. Perhaps you are the one with a plausible solution or a clever invention. Perhaps you are the one meant to assist someone else in developing and implementing a viable plan. In either case, you are a world changer and you can make a difference.

What is your world-changing project for the next year?

_____

_____

_____

_____

_____

_____

_____

What pertinent information must be considered as you develop your PISCO plan?

_____

_____

_____

_____

_____

_____

_____

What are the perceived benefits for people and the organization if this plan is successfully implemented?

_____

_____

_____

_____

_____

_____

_____

"The noblest quest in the world," observed Ben Franklin in _Poor Richard's Almanac_, "is what good may I do in it?"[12]

We challenge you to "get up and get going!" Be a goal achiever but also model servant-leadership by being a "go-giver." If you are already engaged in changing your world, strive to broaden your perspective, deepen your resolve and increase your impact. Even the best can get better.

As world changers, we are called to seize every opportunity to be the best we can be for the world.

I
will
not die
an unlived life.
I will not live in fear
of falling or catching fire.
I choose to inhabit my days,
to allow my living to open me,
to make me less afraid, more accessible,
to loosen my heart until it becomes a wing, a torch,
a promise.
I choose
to risk my significance;
to live so that which came to me
as seed goes to the next as blossom,
and that which came to me as blossom
goes on as fruit.[13] The best has begun.
Always be the
best you can
be for others!

Endnotes

1. *Familiar Quotations*, 300.
2. Stephen Rost, ed., *John Wesley: The Best from All His Works* (Nashville: Thomas Nelson Publishers, 1989).
3. *Six Thinking Hats*, 2.
4. Joe Durant, www.peaksports.com/pdfs/Golfweb_Expectations.pdf (retrieved February 12, 2007).
5. *The Seven Habits of Highly Effective People*, 151.
6. Herbert Taylor, *The Herbert J. Taylor Story* (Downer's Grove, IL: InterVarsity Press, 1968), 41.
7. Marianne Larned, ed., and others, *Stone Soup for the World: Life-Changing Stories of Kindness and Courageous Acts of Service* (Emeryville, CA: Conari Press, 1998), 7.
8. Ibid., 11.
9. Ibid., 401.
10. Ibid., 369.
11. Ibid., 206.
12. Ben Franklin, *Poor Richard's Almanac* (New York: Ballantine Books, 1976).
13. Dawna Markova, *The Open Mind: Discovering the Six Patterns of Natural Intelligence* (Berkeley, California: Conari Press, 1996), 187.

Learning Activities—Chapter 9

To be the best you can be for the world, you must plan your work and work your plan as you passionately pursue your inspired vision.

1. Once you have accomplished a significant goal or milestone in your life it is important to engage in reflection and celebration. Then, it is time to get back to find your next assignment, set the next SMART goal, and engage in the next world-changing project. (A world changing project is simply something where you are trying to solve a problem or pursue an opportunity in helping to make more good things happen in your sphere of influence in the world.) Read chapter 9 and then engage in thinking for constructive change by thoughtfully answering the three questions on pages 208-209. Record thoughtful responses in your Leading Change Journal.

2. Action or transformational learning is about vision, strategy, action (tactics), reflection, change, and accomplishment. If engagement in successful thinking for constructive change and transformational learning experiences produce outstanding results, in what ways are you better today than when you started this study? Record your responses in your Leading Change Journal.

3. Eric Hoffer said, "In times of change the learners inherit the earth, while the learned find themselves equipped to deal with a world that no longer exists." In what ways are you better prepared to inherit the benefits of being a transformational learner as a world changer?

4. Who would you like to mentor or coach through the *Leading Change in Your World* Book Study? Identify these persons and begin your planning.

∽ Notes & Ideas ∽

✎ Notes & Ideas ✎

Works Cited

Barna, George. *Without a Vision, the People Perish—A Barna Report.* Glendale, CA: Barna Research Group Ltd., 1991.

Bartlett, John. *Familiar Quotations.* 5th ed. Boston: Little, Brown and Company, 1955.

Bennis, Warren, and Burt Nanus. *Leaders: The Strategies for Taking Charge.* New York: Harper and Row, 1985.

Bethel, Sheila Murray. *Making a Difference: 12 Qualities that Make You a Leader.* New York: The Berkley Publishing Group, 1990.

Buford, Bob. *Game Plan: Winning Strategies for the Second Half of Your Life.* Grand Rapids: Zondervan Publishing House, 1997.

———. *Half Time: Changing Your Game Plan from Success to Significance.* Grand Rapids: Zondervan Publishing House, 1994.

Carlozo, Louis R. "Achieving Excellence, Family Style." *Life @ Work* 3, no. 2 (March/April 2000): 11.

Celebrating Excellence, Inc. *Celebrating Excellence: Quality, Service, Teamwork, and the Quest for Excellence.* Lombard, IL: Celebrating Excellence Publishing Company, 1992.

Chewning, Richard C., and others. *Business Through the Eyes of Faith.* New York: Harper-Collins Publisher, 1990.

Churchill, Winston. © The Churchill Center, Inc. URL http://www.winstonchurchill.org.

Connor, Patrick E., and Linda K. Lake. *Managing Organizational Change.* New York: Praeger Publishers, 1982.

Covey, Stephen. *The 7 Habits of Highly Effective People: Powerful Lessons in Personal Change.* New York: A Fireside Book, 1990.

De Bono, Edward. *Six Thinking Hats.* Boston: Little, Brown and Company, 1985.

Deen, Edith. *All of the Women of the Bible.* San Francisco: Harper Collins Publishers, 1988.

Deming, W. Edwards. *The New Economics for Industry, Government, Education.* Cambridge, MA: MIT Center for Advanced Engineering Study, 1993.

215

D'Souza, Dinesh. *Ronald Reagan: How an Ordinary Man Became an Extraordinary Leader*. New York: The Free Press, 1997.

Egan, Gerard. *Change Agent Skills B: Managing Innovation and Change*. San Diego: Pfeiffer Publishers, 1988.

Evans, James R., and William M. Lindsay. *The Management and Control of Quality*. St. Paul: West Publishing Company, 1996.

Franklin, Ben. *Poor Richard's Almanac*. New York: Ballantine Books, 1976.

Godwin, Gail. *The Finishing School*. New York: Viking Penguin, 1985. Quoted in Egan, Gerard. *Change Agent Skills B*. San Diego: Pfeiffer Publishers, 1988.

Goleman, Daniel. "Leadership That Gets Results." *Harvard Business Review* (March/April 2000): 78.

Greenleaf, Robert K. *The Servant As Leader*. Indianapolis: The Robert K. Greenleaf Center, 1991.

Hendricks, Howard. *Teaching to Change Lives: Seven Proven Ways to Make Your Teaching Come Alive*. Portland: Multnomah Publishers, 1996.

Holton, Bil. *Leadership Lessons of Robert E. Lee: Tips, Tactics, and Strategies for Leaders and Managers*. New York: Gramercy Books, 1999.

Jones, Laurie Beth. *Jesus CEO*. New York: Hyperion Publishing, 1995.

Katzenback, Jon R., and Douglas Smith. "The Discipline of Teams." *Harvard Business Review* (March/April 1993): 111-20.

———. *The Wisdom of Teams: Creating the High-Performance Organization*. Watertown, MA: Harvard Business School Press, 1993.

Kotter, John P. *Leading Change*. Boston: Harvard Business School Press, 1996.

Kouzes, James M., and Barry Z. Posner. *The Leadership Challenge: How to Keep Getting Extraordinary Things Done in Organizations*. From The Jossey-Bass Management Series. San Francisco: Jossey-Bass Publishers, 1995.

Larned, Marianne, ed., and others. *Stone Soup for the World: Life-Changing Stories of Kindness and Courageous Acts of Service*. Emeryville, CA: Conari Press, 1998.

Laub, Jim. *Assessing the Servant Organization: A description of the six key areas and eighteen characteristics of the Servant Organization*. Jim Laub ©2000.

WORKS CITED

Laurence, Peter J. *Peter's Quotations: Ideas for Our Time*. New York: Bantam Books, 1977.

Lewin, Kurt. *Field Theory in Social Science*. Edited by D. Cartwright. New York: Harper and Row Brokers, 1951.

Logsdon, Tom. *Breaking Through*. New York: Addison-Wesley Publishing House, 1993.

Markova, Dawna. *The Open Mind: Discovering the Six Patterns of Natural Intelligence*. Berkeley, CA: Conari Press, 1996.

Maxwell, John. *The 21 Irrefutable Laws of Leadership*. Nashville: Thomas Nelson, 1998.

Moorhead, Gregory, and Ricky W. Griffin. *Organizational Behavior: Managing People and Organizations*. Boston: Houghton Mifflin, 1998.

Moran, Linda, ed. Ed Musselwhite and John H. Zenger, contributors. *Keeping Teams on Track: What to Do When the Going Gets Rough*. Toronto, Ontario: Irwin Professional Publications, 1996.

Muggeridge, Malcolm. *Something Beautiful for God: Mother Teresa of Calcutta*. Garden City, NY: Image Books, 1977.

Nichols, James O. *A Practitioner's Handbook for Institutional Effectiveness and Student Outcomes Assessment Implementation*. 3rd edition. Edison, NJ: Agathon Press, 1996.

Penticuff, Dave, ed. Quoting Jim Barnes in "Integrity, Moral Character Critical in a Leader." Marion, Indiana: *Chronicle-Tribune* (June 4, 2000).

Romig, Dennis. *Breakthrough Teamwork: Outstanding Results Using Structured Teamwork*. Chicago: Performance Research Press, 1999.

Rosen, Robert H., with Lisa Berger. *The Healthy Company: Eight Strategies to Develop People, Productivity, and Profits*. Los Angeles: Jeremy P. Tarcher, Inc., 1991.

Roth, David. *Sacred Honor: A Biography of Colin Powell*. Grand Rapids: Zondervan Publishing House, 1993.

Schwann, Charles J., and others. *Total Leaders: Applying the Best Future-Focused Change Strategies to Education*. AASA Distribution Center, 1998.

Senge, Peter, ed., and others. *The Fifth Discipline Fieldbook: Strategies and Tools for Building a Learning Organization*. New York: Currency/Doubleday, 1994.

Shonk, James H. *Team Based Organizations: Developing a Successful Team Environment.* Toronto, Ontario: Irwin Professional Publications, 1997.

Taylor, Herbert. *The Herbert J. Taylor Story.* Downer's Grove, IL: InterVarsity Press, 1968.

Ziglar, Zig. *See You at the Top.* Gretna, LA: Pelican Publishing Company, 1982.

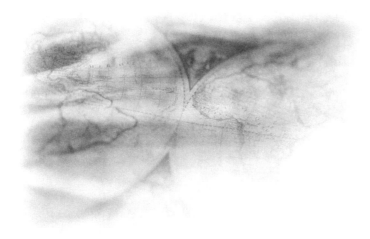

Index

About the Authors

Larry Lindsay, Ed.D., presently serves as the Executive Assistant to the President (Chief of Staff) of Indiana Wesleyan University. Dr. Lindsay joined the faculty and administration of Indiana Wesleyan in 1995. He led the transformation of the Masters in Education Program from 1995-1998. Larry then served as the Founding Chair of the School Leadership Program and the Founding Chair of the Department of Leadership in leading the development of the Doctorate in Organizational Leadership. As a full professor he has taught in the M.Ed., MSM, MBA, School Leadership, and Organizational Leadership programs.

In 2001 Dr. Lindsay was recognized as the national faculty recipient of the Paul E. Hoffner Outstanding Service Award for the Consortium for the Advancement of Adult Higher Education. In 2002 he was recognized as the faculty recipient for the Indiana Wesleyan University President's Meritorious Service Award.

Dr. Lindsay served for four years as the Vice President of Positive Life Attitudes for America, the educational division of the Zig Ziglar Corporation in Dallas, Texas. At the Zig Ziglar Corporation, he led the educational division, wrote curriculum and training materials, designed and facilitated numerous seminars, trained instructor/facilitators, taught in Born to Win Seminars and conducted workshops throughout America. He continues to serve as an instructional designer and organizational leadership consultant to schools and businesses as a facilitator of LeaderThink.

Dr. Lindsay served as the superintendent/headmaster of a K-12 Christian college preparatory school in Dallas from 1985-1995. Previously he served as assistant superintendent of schools in the Metropolitan School District (MSD) of Wayne Township (Ben Davis High School) and the MSD of Washington Township (North Central High School) in the Greater Indianapolis area for seven years.

Mark A. Smith, Ed.D., is the President of Ohio Christian University. He has published numerous articles and book chapters and is a frequent speaker at educational conferences. In October 2003, Dr. Smith accepted an appointment to President George W. Bush's board for the Fund for the Improvement of Postsecondary Education.

After completing his undergraduate work at Hobe Sound Bible College, Dr. Smith graduated from West Virginia University with a doctorate in higher education administration. Whether as teacher, principal, or administrator, his career has focused on leadership and planning. He has instituted college-wide assessment programs in several colleges, and worked with school corporations, colleges, civic organizations, and corporate students to promote vision casting and strategic planning. Throughout his career, Dr. Smith has piloted many teams, helping them to navigate the complex issues that organizations today confront.

Dr. Smith has been involved in ministry for several years, serving as a Pastor and Assistant District Superintendent in The Wesleyan Church.

Dr. Smith is a consultant evaluator for the North Central Association of Colleges. Mark has one purpose for this book, summed up in this thought: "You can change your world."